Transforming Charity
Toward a Results-Oriented Social Sector

URBAN CHURCH
LEADERSHIP CENTER
3000 Leonard NE - 2nd Level/GRTS
Grand Rapids, MI 49525

Transforming Charity
Toward a Results-Oriented Social Sector

by
Ryan Streeter

Indianapolis, Indiana

Transforming Charity: Toward a Results-Oriented Social Sector
Ryan Streeter
ISBN 1-55813-131-0
$16.95

Copyright © 2001 Hudson Institute, Inc.

All rights reserved. No part of this publication may be reproduced, by any process or technique, without the express written consent of the publisher, except in the case of brief quotations embodied in critical articles and reviews.

The views in this book are solely the views of the author. No opinions, statements of fact, or conclusions contained in this document can be properly attributed to Hudson Institute, its staff, its members, its contracted agencies, or the other institutions with which the author is affiliated.

Printed in the United States of America.

For information about obtaining additional copies of this or other Hudson Institute publications, contact:

Hudson Institute Publications
P.O. Box 486
Westfield, IN 46074
Toll-free: 888-554-1325
Fax: 317-867-0725
Or, visit Hudson's online bookstore at http://www.hudson.org.

For media and speaking engagement purposes, contact Hudson at 317-545-1000 or via the Internet at info@hudson.org or speakers@hudson.org.

CONTENTS

PREFACE 9
CHAPTER ONE: NEW CHARITY, CIVIL SOCIETY, AND THE FUTURE 15
   Seeing the New Charity in the Past: Emden's Social Welfare 15
   Surfing in the Wake of Welfare Reform 19
      Welfare Reform and the Civil Society Movement 23
      A Multisector Strategy 26
      Three Questions in Search of Three Answers 33
   Intentions versus Investments 35
      What Does American Generosity Mean? 36
      New Charity in the United States 38
      Beyond Bickering about Social Capital 41
   Three Important Domains 44
CHAPTER TWO: WHERE THE MISSION MEETS THE MARKET 51
   Blurring the Lines between Social and Commercial 51
      Mission and Market at the Individual and Organizational Levels 53
   Jobs Partnership 57
      Getting People to Work through a Program That Works 58
      A Holistic Program 60
   ServiceMaster's Work Training Businesses 63
      Producing Economic and Social Value 64
      Case Study: Chicago Christian Industrial League 66
      Capacity Building 70
      The Mission, the Market, and the Future 72
   The Roberts Enterprise Development Fund-a New Breed of Investor 74
      Creating Social Returns on Investment 74
      Case Study: Community Vocational Enterprises 77
   Conclusion: What the Public Sector Should Be Doing with All of This .. 79
      Government the Coordinator 80
      Government the Investor 81

CHAPTER THREE: BUILDING A CIVIC INFRASTRUCTURE BY
LEVERAGING LOCAL INTERMEDIARIES 85
   The Pillars of Civic Infrastructure 86
   Whose Job Is It to Help Those Left Behind? 92
   Between the Heavenly City and the Earthly City:
      Intermediary Organizers 98
      The Effective Community Intermediary:
         Ottawa County Good Samaritan *102*
      Government Facilitator: The Front Porch Alliance *109*
   Post-Welfare Reform and a Strong Civic Infrastructure *115*
CHAPTER FOUR: TOWARD A HIGH-IMPACT SOCIAL SECTOR *127*
   Social Spending in America *127*
   Social Investment in America *130*
   Measuring Return on Investment *137*
      ROI-T *139*
      ROI-D *139*
      ROI-E *140*
      Social Return on Investment-REDF Again *141*
   Conclusion *150*
      New Ways *151*
      Where Do the New Ways Take Us? *153*
ABOUT HUDSON INSTITUTE *161*
INDEX *163*

"The best philanthropy, the help that does the most good and the least harm, the help that nourishes civilization at its very root, that most widely disseminates health, righteousness, and happiness, is not what is usually called charity."
John D. Rockefeller, Sr., *The Wise Art of Giving*

"We make a living by what we get. We make a life by what we give."
Winston Churchill

"Equal neglect is not impartial kindness. The species of benevolence which arises from contempt is no true charity."
Edmund Burke, *Reflections on the Revolution in France*

TRANSFORMING CHARITY

PREFACE

There are two types of people in the world: those who routinely divide everyone into two types, and those who don't. The former risk oversimplifying things to make a point, which is what I will do to characterize this book: there are those who admire a charitable act because of what it intends, and there are those that admire it because of its results. This bifurcation is nothing new.

Take the Jewish practice of *tzedakah*, for instance. For centuries, Jewish households and communities have cared for the poor in their midst because of the obligation placed upon them by *tzedakah*, or charity. The Jewish idea of charity holds that the highest form of help for the less fortunate respects their dignity by freeing them from the need to beg and helping them become self-reliant. This may happen through a loan, assistance in finding a job, or a mentoring relationship. This understanding of charity upholds the dignity of the person in need and has little to do with more popular understandings of "charity" that suggest magnanimity or a generous heart. *Tzedakah's* Hebrew root means righteousness, or justice. It has to do with treating poor individuals justly, and in its highest form, this means enabling them to rise above poverty and remain there. It has a result in mind and has little to do with the intentions of the donor.

Contrast the Jewish notion of charity with the following quote from an early modern poet: "Charity is a virtue of the heart. Gifts and alms are the expressions, not the essence, of this virtue." This view of charity holds that helping those left behind is really all about intentions. The heart justifies the giving. This predominant view of assisting the poor has made even egregious expressions of intention-based giving seem like common sense to many, such as this rather banal maxim I recently heard: "Happiness is not so much in having as in sharing." While it is true that happiness is often a pleasant byproduct of giving, my happiness about my giving does not make my giving good or smart. Only results can do that. If I give and volunteer mainly to appease a guilty conscience or to convince myself and others I am "doing good" or to have a "cause" to support, I am missing the point and probably giving irresponsibly. But even if I give unselfishly out of a heartfelt concern for the poor while remaining unaware of or careless about what is actually resulting from my "charity," am I really giving more responsibly? Or if I give to my favorite organizations because "they're such good people" without knowing much about what those good people are actually achieving, what does that say about my concern for the populations they serve? Much of what passes for assistance to families in need is rooted in an understanding of charity that says giving is justified so long as the intentions behind it are good. That someone would give merely to be happy is an extreme expression of this kind of charity, but it is not much different than all forms of intention-based charity, which focus too heavily on the act of giving and too little on the effects of the giving.

Intention-based charity becomes particularly harmful when it becomes the modus operandi of foundations, charities, and government agencies. Foundations pack their glossy annual reports with pictures of the people their dollars have helped, with neat anecdotes in sidebars to boot. Charities take up a cause and solicit funds from people who feel good about having a cause to give to. Governments spend great time and energy, not to mention money, designing a legion of programs affecting low-income communities, and then spend even more inspecting the programs' processes rather than real outcomes. Who loses in an intention-based world where results are largely neglected? If ineffective charity becomes too hard to ignore, philanthropists may grow a bit more frustrated, taxpayers may fret more about big, wasteful government, and those who find happiness in sharing more and having less may just be less happy. But none of them really loses much of anything. It is those we claim to be helping that get hurt the most.

This book considers "charity" quite broadly to mean assistance to the less fortunate, especially those facing barriers to sustained employment. The book is less concerned with whether or not the charity is "pure" in the sense that it is private and given of a free will. What it is concerned with is whether or not charity is intention-based or investment-based, regardless if the resources come from private or public sources. Investment-based charity, to borrow from the world of finance, wants to see positive results. Recent stock market woes in America have accentuated the point that people investing in companies showing zero or negative profitability—namely, those not producing results—are among the most disappointed investors. Investment-based charity, likewise, is oriented toward results. It wants to see that it is creating value in some identifiable way. And no cause is worthy enough to justify a gift that is not making a truly positive difference in the lives of those for whom it is intended.

This book looks at charitable practices that take results seriously. It is particularly concerned with charitable activity aimed at helping those in various forms of dependency reach at least economic independence and, hopefully, overall well-being. And in today's world, to take results seriously means that we have to take the institutions of civil society seriously. We are seeing more and more donors and deliverers of services to low-income families talk favorably, even desirously, about producing higher levels of effectiveness in their charitable enterprises. At the same time, the forces of devolution are demanding higher levels of performance at the grass-roots. The institutions of civil society, which consist mainly of nonprofit organizations and other forms of association working for, in and through communities, are the key to increasing effectiveness while handling the demands of devolution. But they cannot do this well without creative partnerships. And because civil society stands or falls on its ability to make productive relationships happen in a community, investment-based charity will likely stand or fall on the quality of the local institutions of civil society.

Relationships at the interpersonal and organizational levels are crucial to the success of our efforts to help others.

Charity, in this book, is therefore discussed less in terms of the distinct causes for the sake of which charitable dollars and services are delivered than in terms of the environment in which they are delivered. What kind of "civic infrastructure" are local business, civic, and government leaders fostering in their communities? How well do the different sectors work together? How do they know if they are succeeding? Federal resources and foundation grants flow equally into a number communities but produce radically different results. It is not the resources themselves that account for the difference but the relational environments in which they are deployed. Relationship-building is key to community-building. If we do not get a variety of actors working together in new ways for the benefit of our (especially low-income) communities, the resources we send into those communities will have far less than their potential impact.

Chapter One takes a look at investment-based charity against the backdrop of welfare reform in America in the 1990s and the movement to take civil society seriously. The chapter concludes that effective, investment-based charity will be helped by bringing market actors and charitable institutions more closely together, learning how to harness the positive energy of multiple community-based assets through intermediaries, and creating new standards for assessing results. Chapters Two through Four showcase leading examples of each of these three elements.

It is claimed more than once in the book that these examples do not exhaust the range of possibilities for transforming charity from its intention-based to results-oriented manifestations. But the examples do represent the kinds of activity that hold great promise for the future of American charity, especially if we concentrate our attention on their replication and expansion.

The ideas in this book are hardly my own, though I take full responsibility for the way they are presented. The greatest benefit in writing a book such as this is the people one meets along the way. Getting to know so many individuals and communities doing such great work is a lesson in the power of humanity. It also inspires confidence in the future of American citizenship. I cannot thank everyone who has affected the spirit of this book, but I will take time to acknowledge those who have directly shaped its contents and fundamental ideas.

My thanks are due first to Jay Hein, who originally conceived this book and began as its co-author. Without his insight and input, the book would not have been realized. If it is possible to be a co-author without getting your name on the cover, then that is the role Jay has played. He was ahead of the curve in understanding how much the success of welfare reform in America would depend on the kind of charity discussed in this book. Amy Sherman has not only introduced me to some of the people and ideas I write about in Chapters Two and Three, but her immense productivity as a scholar and practitioner of life-transforming charity has greatly challenged me. Curt Smith never lets me forget the indispensable role that civil society's institutions play and has encouraged me to grow more sophisticated in the way I think about their effects on society in general.

Don Eberly, perhaps the most humane spokesman of civic renewal in America, has offered me valuable feedback on the manuscript and has inspired me to think through the significance of themes I have left unexplored in this book. Steve Goldsmith has shown me more than anyone that caring about community-based organizations and the people they serve cannot be separated from caring about results. Herb London read the entire manuscript and provided valuable comments.

My early thoughts on the topics in this book were helpfully influenced through conversations with Paul Brooks, who first made me think about the untapped magnitude of the social sector, and with Lenore Ealy, who helped expand my appreciation for the historical importance of civic institutions.

Bill Bedrossian's input helped improve Chapter Two, and his commitment to the mission and the market has served to transform lives and inspire my work. Skip Long, Chris Mangum, David Spickard, and James White supplied helpful information and comments on the text. Their commitment to the less fortunate and to healing some of the more painful fissures that exist between people, were we able to reproduce it, would leave our children a world whose beauty we would scarcely recognize.

Isaac Randolph and Bill Stanczykiewicz showed me first-hand how a city successfully goes about building an alliance out of hundreds of front porches. And a good number of Indianapolis pastors and neighborhood leaders—most notably, Frank Alexander, Charles Harrison, Jay Height, Tim Streett, and Olgen Williams—have shown me how powerful those front porches can be. Janet De Young was most helpful in supplying information and comments for Chapter Three.

Jed Emerson, whose idiosyncratic, forward-looking style infuses everything he does, has inspired important aspects of Chapters Two and Four. If anything appears idiosyncratic and forward-looking in the text, it must mean that Jed's ideas are rubbing off on my rather mainstream and backward-looking disposition. Dennis Benson, who confirms that idiosyncratic vision is a virtue of people who spend their time worrying about how to measure returns on social investments, has provided valuable comments on the manuscript and has encouraged me to think rigorously about social impact.

Melinda Tuan and Julia Jones have supplied very helpful recommendations for improving Chapter Four. Maureen Lee, Chris Mann, Karyn Traphagen, and Maki Wiering cleaned up various parts of the manuscript and turned it into the final product.

And, most importantly, my wife Kathryn's enduring love keeps my feet firmly planted on the ground while at the same time inspiring me to go ever higher.

CHAPTER ONE
New Charity, Civil Society, and the Future

Seeing the New Charity in the Past: Emden's Social Welfare

More than four hundred years ago in now-forgotten Emden, a northern German port city, history was being made. This little city, known as "the Geneva of the north" in its day, became an affluent commercial center during the time Reformed Calvinist doctrine was establishing itself in its ecclesiastical and civic institutions. The conflicts between the Netherlands and Spain in the mid-sixteenth century resulted in a vast flight of Dutch wealth and talent to this welcoming city. The influx of new people also brought large numbers of poor immigrants. The city, like most European cities before the Reformation, had a tradition of decentralized charity, headed up by the Church's mendicant orders and other ecclesiastical clerics and based upon a theology of good works, in which the benefactors of poor relief found their reward-in this life and the next-through the goodness of giving itself. Beggars were common and were usually not discouraged from their begging. The practice of charity placed few, if any, conditions on the continual receipt of financial assistance.[1]

But with the Reformation came a radical shift in caring for the poor in Emden. Considered harsh by many of its critics, poor relief in the city began to place conditions upon the receipt of charity. Begging was forbidden—nothing was to be got for nothing. Poor parents were to see to it that their children took advantage of publicly provided education as a condition for receiving financial assistance. Poor relief was centralized in the local public administration, while its distribution was decentralized to lay members (rather than clerics) of the church, many of whom were merchants and tradesmen.

By the year 1600, Emden's social welfare system was as respectable as its commercial success. While public welfare funds originated mainly from the collection of fines and temporarily levied taxes, Emden's citizens gave generously-so much so that the Reformed church accountant in 1590 complained that they were giving too much and thus making the job of accounting for their gifts difficult. Two historically significant shifts took place during the last fifty years of the sixteenth century as welfare was reformed in the city.

The humanization of the poor.

The reformers contended that the old form of charity, while honorable in intentions, actually kept the poor in poverty. However pure it looked on the outside, it was fairly sinister. To keep beggars poor so that charity has an "object" is cruel, the reformers claimed. Even the poor could become self-supporting citizens and productive members of the social order. Begging was outlawed, not so that officials could have a reason to beat up on the poor (and in good Calvinist fashion, beggars were in fact beaten!), but to force the poor to participate in new welfare programs that would train them in the benefits of virtuous action and economic self-sufficiency. "Poor wardens," or people we call caseworkers today, were tasked with supervising the poor to make sure that they were not wasting alms on such things as drinking and carousing. Poor residents, particularly vagrant beggars who had wandered to Emden, were assigned to workhouses where they were taught the value of work and closely supervised.

Juan Luis Vives, an early-sixteenth-century humanist who favored such reforms wrote that they "will not prevent a man from becoming a pauper but will prevent him from remaining long in that condition, by promptly stretching forth a hand to help him to his feet."[2] In our world, this has been called giving "hand-ups" rather than handouts. He also says that the poor would be "restored to themselves" through the process:

CHAPTER ONE

> *[The poor] . . . will live among men like citizens, disciplined, observant of human laws; they will keep their hands pure from acts of violence; they will serve God truly and honestly; they will be men; they will be what they are called, Christians.* [3]

For the new poor-relief system, the education of poor youth was perhaps the signature weapon against poverty. "Preventive measures," as we call them, were the reformers' main focus. Reformed Protestants were often humanists when it came to education, and they saw schooling as the process whereby citizens were formed and prepared to contribute to public life and welfare. Inculcating virtue and equipping young people with vocational skills were the two fundamental forms of insurance against poverty.

The motivation for reforming welfare in sixteenth-century Emden, a city where one-fifth of the population received some form of welfare assistance in 1570 due to the great influx of immigrants, was as much a desire for civic health and economic prosperity as it was a zeal for religious piety. To this end, the city needed productive, engaged citizens. And while the sixteenth-century solutions of strict discipline and punishment for poor people strike twenty-first-century ears as cruel, the reform efforts were propelled by a confidence that the poor could become nonpoor-that they could be "restored to themselves"—dignified and capable human beings.

Reformed and effective institutions.

Before the sixteenth-century welfare reforms, caring for the poor was largely the job of various orders within the church according to local needs. The reforms brought with them the placement of social welfare work within the civil administration, where it could be centralized and rationalized according to specific conditions, which placed expectations upon the poor, outlined the task of the poor wardens, and required an account of how poor relief was spent. But this act of centralization did not produce a bureaucracy. The administration of poor relief was in part the responsibility of communities within the city, and lay members took over the job, often as deacons of the Reformed Protestant church. Guild entrance fees, once given to the Catholic Church, went to the civil magistrates as well as the "godly poor" (low-income, working individuals) within a guild's network. Guilds were also ordered to set aside for the poor in their midst the money that they usually spent on excessive drinking and feasting. Rather than relegating the care of the poor to clerics of the church, as was formerly the practice, poor citizens were to become members of communities that had the responsibility of caring for them. Brotherhoods, or confraternities, survived from medieval practice and became the "mission arm" of merchants and tradesmen in Reformed Emden. These brotherhoods organized themselves to take in able-bodied poor workers, train them in a trade, and support them until they could become self-supporting. The lines between the market activities and the social mission of these brotherhoods were far blurrier than they are in our world.

Another important reform was that of making more concise distinctions between various kinds of poverty. Formerly, the poor, usually beggars, were lumped into one class. So long as they were begging, they were in need of aid. The new social welfare in Emden drew lines between the marginally poor and the truly poor, the latter being those who faced significant barriers to self-reliant living. The simple criterion was whether or not someone was able-bodied enough to work and be a part of society. There were no government-determined "poverty thresholds." Because the care of the poor was situated in locally responsible communities, those who needed help could be identified fairly easily.

As a historical phenomenon, Emden serves as a prototype for what we observe in American society today. Emden became a city that was concerned with "transforming charity"—both in the sense of charity that transforms its recipients and with regard to the transformation of the institutions of charitable activity. What characterized Emden's poor relief is remarkably similar to the spirit of welfare reform in the United States during the 1990s:

> 1. *The belief that good intentions themselves do not justify charitable acts.* Welfare reform in America is part of a larger trend that has come to regard the mere disbursement of money to "relieve" suf-

fering as an ineffective—and sometimes even irresponsible—
method for lifting the poor out of poverty. Consensus has begun
to form around the notion that the results of giving are what
make charity legitimate or not. Giving that hurts people–or just
keeps them poor—over the long term is "bad charity," regardless
of intentions.

2. *An intolerance for largely "condition-less" relationships between the poor and the benefactor, between service provider and benefactor.* In Emden, the view of begging moved from acceptable to taboo. While welfare reform in the United States has had nothing directly to do with begging, a similar taboo has been erected against the notion of getting aid without working in return. The "nothing is got for nothing" principle has been placed in the forefront of the welfare and social services reform efforts of the past decade. This principle also applies to the accountability relationship between the provider of services and the provider of the financial resources for the services.

3. *Greater community participation.* While Emden centralized the administration of poor relief in the sixteenth century, service delivery was diversified to include "nonprofessionals," or nontraditional providers. Emden's reforms began to include communities and businesspeople in poor relief. In a devolutionary way, recent welfare reform efforts in America have shifted the onus of responsibility for caring for the poor from primarily government to communities as a whole—meaning both government agencies and private participants such as employers and community-based organizations.

Surfing in the Wake of Welfare Reform

America is in the middle of a much larger and more complex experiment than Emden's, but which embodies the principles of the city's social welfare reforms. We are witnessing a growing impatience among many actors in the social sector about the way that public and private relief to families in need is often executed with good intentions but without results-oriented practices in place. We also see accountability discussed in mantra-like fashion at all levels of human services, though actual accountability and performance practices vary widely depending on region and agency. And we have watched the number of "players" in social welfare multiply due to the state and federal welfare reform effort of the 1990s. Government no longer has the primary responsibility for poor relief; entire communities do. This is creating a historical change, the effects of which we are only beginning to feel.

Charity, broadly understood as assistance to the poor, is being transformed in America. And this transformation is occurring in two main areas. First, organizations that serve low-income and indigent populations, both religious and secular, public and private, are discovering the central importance of personal transformation in their clients. There has been a growing consensus over the past two decades that it is difficult to separate the facts of homelessness, teen pregnancy, welfare dependency, and a range of social pathologies from the personal beliefs and habits that are at least partially responsible for these phenomena. Academics, policy makers, and community leaders are less inclined today than they were during a large portion of the twentieth century to locate root causes of poverty in institutions and large-scale social structures alone, but in the value-related practices of people as well. The recent acceptance by liberals and conservatives alike of faith-based organizations as legitimate providers of publicly funded social programs is perhaps the best example of this changing framework. The strength of FBOs, as they have come to be known, is in their power to transform the lives of the people with whom they work. Charity that transforms poverty-promoting habits into poverty-beating habits—and does not simply deliver services out of clearly stated good intentions—is of interest to a society that increasingly demands optimal use of its financial resources. It is also of interest to a society that claims some ways of living are better than others.

CHAPTER ONE

The subject of habits is more than hypothetical. For example, in a recent report studying trends in American economic inequality, the U.S. Census Bureau attributes the cause of growing inequality in part to changes in family structure and living arrangements. While the report cites such important factors as the downward trend in wages among the less-educated workforce, it also says that "increases in divorces and separations, increases in births out of wedlock, and the increasing age at first marriage may have all led to a shift away from traditionally higher-income married-couple households and toward lower-income single-parent nonfamily households."[4] Not long ago, such explanations were considered biased, reactionary responses by conservative moralists. Now, a general consensus has emerged that one of the best ways to combat poverty is to help people overcome the habits and kinds of choices that will almost guarantee them a life of poverty.

Second, the recognition of the first point—that the best charity is that which transforms habits—has led to new expectations among providers of charitable services and resources. It is becoming increasingly difficult to justify charity by an appeal to the good intentions of the funders and service providers or a show of the numbers of people served. People want to see a charity's measurable impact. While very few tools for measuring social impact currently exist, sentiments for better performance in charitable activity are growing and have given birth to alternative philanthropic lifestyles. "Social entrepreneurs" and "venture philanthropy" have arisen as names for those who apply market principles to socially redeeming enterprises. But numerous foundations and innovative individuals, not to mention state and federal government agencies, have begun to implement strategies for producing results in the social sector. Less concerned with designing and funding massive programs, they are focusing upon methods for producing lasting change among the recipients of their services, many of which are grassroots, locally managed efforts in which the level of attention given to clients is substantial.

The increased emphasis placed on results by public and private funding communities is forcing nonprofit organizations to reconsider their work in terms of the results they produce. A study by Christine Letts, William Ryan, and Allen Grossman concluded that the greatest contributor to a nonprofit's ability for social impact is organizational capacity. However, most nonprofits have conventionally tried to increase their effectiveness by expanding programs, spreading information about best practices and effective innovations, or reforming policy.[5] These do not affect outcomes or an organization's capacity to manage its work, define and reach targets, and so on. As charitable organizations are called upon to give a greater account for their social impact than in times past, they will need to take capacity-building seriously. They are realizing that productivity matters to the suppliers of their resources and, as noted management author Jim Collins says, "well-managed corporate entities—be they for-profit or not-for-profit—have become the dominant productive vehicle in society."[6] The growing recognition of this need to strengthen administrative and operational capacity is already giving birth to a brand-new services industry that makes nonprofit capacity-building its central task. For instance, Bain and Company, a $700 million Boston strategic consulting firm, has created The Bridge Group, a nonprofit organization that makes use of Bain's top talent (for up to 80 percent less their normal salaries) to provide strategic consulting to nonprofits. "There simply is no force to push consolidations and to move organizations to an appropriate scale to fulfill their mission," says Thomas J. Tierney, Bain's worldwide managing director and founder of The Bridge Group.[7]

"Transforming charity" thus has a double meaning. It refers to the kind of assistance that helps people facing barriers to the economic and social mainstream to transform their lives. It also refers to the way in which charitable practices, or services to the poor in general, are being transformed from an intention-based, process-focused framework to one that is results-based. This period of transformation, not without coincidence, parallels the effort in America to reform our wasteful welfare systems. This in turn parallels a broader movement over the past twenty-five years to strengthen "civil society," or that aspect of society in which citizens take individual and collective responsibility for the condition of their lives and communities.

CHAPTER ONE

Welfare Reform and the Civil Society Movement

Welfare reform in the United States was much broader than the federal Personal Responsibility and Work Opportunity Reconciliation Act of 1996, which replaced the old welfare system by giving states block grants and almost sole authority in designing their plans for moving people from welfare to work. It was part of a larger cultural movement that had grown suspicious of attempts to cure social ills absent the vigorous participation of localities and citizens themselves. Welfare reform arguably became the single greatest experiment in public policy in the latter half of the twentieth century. It gave localities a greater stake in a significant social problem, while at the same time, it embodied a new moral consensus in legislation. The law, candidly described, was based on the idea that habits promoting work were better for people than habits encouraging nonwork and financial dependence upon public coffers.

Welfare reform began in a number of forward-looking states that were seeking how to move away from an entitlement culture where it was not unusual for some welfare recipients to receive cash assistance for more than ten years. The arguments for welfare reform were as much social—even moral—as they were financial. Welfare bureaucracies were expensive, indeed, but they also fostered reliance on continued assistance, which prolonged poverty and demoralized recipients and their children. Successful welfare reform, it was argued, would be based on the idea that people who could work should work, and that public assistance should be designed to serve this end.

Thus it is unfortunate that our current measures of "success" focus too heavily upon a largely economic factor—that is, welfare reform is often currently praised in virtue of its reduction of welfare caseloads, which purportedly reduces the financial cost to government. It is no doubt significant that between August 1996, and December 1999, the welfare caseload in America dropped from 12.2 million individuals to 6.2 million, or 49 percent.[8] States have exceeded even the most optimistic projections about their capacity to move people from welfare to work. Because of their efforts and a favorable economy, the percentage of people receiving public assistance is the lowest it has been since 1967, which is remarkable given the fact that in 1994 it was at its highest point in the nation's history.

Nevertheless, the degree to which former recipients are on a track toward a baseline economic citizenship—in which they are increasing their standard of living, paying taxes and consuming fewer tax dollars in the form of received services over time—is what should be assessed, though it is not being systematically done.[9] We know that in 1999 poverty rates for all racial and ethnic groups, especially African Americans, reached or equaled historic lows—evidence that programs encouraging work over welfare are themselves working.[10] The new concern at the state level, though, is that more and more public resources are needed to provide supportive services to those who are working but are still poor. Wisconsin, for instance, spends less than 20 percent of its public assistance on direct cash assistance to families; the rest is used to pay for supportive services such as transportation, child care, and so on for working poor families. Whether or not our public and private interventions are helping people acquire the stability they need to move out of these new yet still publicly funded environments is our most pressing poverty issue today. And how well we equip people to advance in careers is what we need to be assessing.

But this raises larger social and moral questions: Are former welfare recipients forming the relationships and developing the habits and skills that they need to become contributing members of society? Is it worth continuing reforms to carry out this social goal even if the initial financial costs are the same—or higher—than the costs of the old system?

The social and moral component evident within welfare reform argumentation and rhetoric was part of a larger cultural movement to foster greater independence among individuals and communities over against impersonal and inefficient bureaucracies. Widely read works such as *The Quest for Community*, written by Robert Nisbet in 1953, and *To Empower People*, written by Peter Berger and Richard John Neuhaus in 1977, argued that Americans needed to increase the value of voluntary organizations and other significant mediating institutions such as families, neighborhood-serving organizations, and religious organizations—all of which strengthen primarily local democratic life in the face of the large and impersonal agencies of the federal government.[11] This larger movement that focused upon revitalizing "civil society" ran in tandem with the growing effort to reform welfare. Nontraditional private-sector service providers, businesses, and FBOs have all been called upon to make our social welfare mechanisms both more economical and more morally vibrant. In sum, the movement's focus has been to engage citizens more directly in solving our most-pressing social problems and in shaping our public life in general. The civil society movement has a twofold significance on our society's care for the poor. First, the greater emphasis on responsible citizenship has made it seem more socially aberrant for someone capable of earning his or her own living to be dependent on publicly funded services. Second, the civil-society movement's emphasis on increased responsibility and activity on the part of local community-based organizations has translated into an expanded, locally - driven network of care for the poor.

This movement has touched policy makers in the nation's statehouses, as well as in Washington, and has created greater problem-solving activity in localities. Several examples are worth mentioning. The "responsible fatherhood movement" has resulted in numerous programs across the nation focused upon reconnecting fathers—especially those who are low-income—with their children. Recent attempts have been made to enact federal legislation that would encourage the replication and growth of these programs.

Through the 1996 welfare reform act, the federal government has reached out to FBOs through its Charitable Choice clause, allowing them to receive federal dollars to assist in the welfare reform effort without sacrificing their religious character. It has become a model for a number of pending bills from housing to crime fighting. And the most recent data suggests that the 1996 law has created a substantial ripple effect by encouraging the start-up of many new government collaborations with the faith community, many of which are nonfinancial collaborations.[12] And an impressive number of these collaborations involve small organizations, suggesting that the "little guy" closest to the population in need is getting in the game.

The past two decades have seen a substantial growth in the activity of community development corporations (CDCs), which concentrate all of their grant-making on community development initiatives, be they "bricks and mortar" or human services projects. The roughly four thousand CDCs in America truly are community assets, for they invest in their neighborhoods and are managed by local residents. A new phenomenon in the community development movement is the growing interest in individual development accounts (IDAs), which represent the effort to grow the assets of low-income families. A complete departure from the entitlement mindset, IDAs are a "bootstrap effort" that encourage work, savings, education, and enterprise.[13]

A Multisector Strategy

All of these examples are indicators of a significant cultural change that is underway. And they demonstrate how the increased emphasis on "civil society" is resulting in new policy and practice aimed at improving the condition of poor Americans. At the level of individuals and families, the first domain of transformed charity, this cultural change can be felt in the growing societal expectation that citizens be as responsible for their lives as possible. It can also be seen in a growing awareness that organizations capable of helping others in this way should be more greatly involved in public welfare efforts than they have been in recent history. Private community-based organizations, FBOs, and even corporations should at least make a concerted effort—if not form a partnership—with public agencies whenever their social missions overlap. There is general agreement among policy makers and practitioners that the complexity of solving social problems in today's line-blurring world is moving us toward a *multisector approach* in addressing social issues. The three major sectors in such an approach are government, business, and private nonprofit organizations.

Almost every leading example of organizations that are strengthening civil society, particularly with respect to services targeted to the poor,

CHAPTER ONE

involve more than one sector. In a world of transforming charity, problems are generally too complex for one sector to solve alone. If poverty is as much a moral as economic issue, then neither the government, nor the business, nor the nonprofit sectors can address it by themselves. Most civil society advocates characterize civil society mainly as the realm of the nonprofit sector. This does not seem entirely accurate. A world of transforming charity requires multisector problem-solving, and in so far as these multisector efforts are strengthening citizenship and communities, it is difficult to distinguish them from civil society. The ends of civil society—engaged citizens, active and responsible associations, and a humane culture—are often achieved through multisector collaborations, and so long as it is the ends we care about, then the sectors involved should not be of great concern. One caveat is in order, though: almost every successful multisector collaboration is local. Chapters Two and Three examine effective multisector programs and initiatives, each of which is local. The degree to which national multisector initiatives strengthen civil society of their own accord, or at least improve the condition of the poor, is not yet clear.

We can represent the multiple sectors as follows:

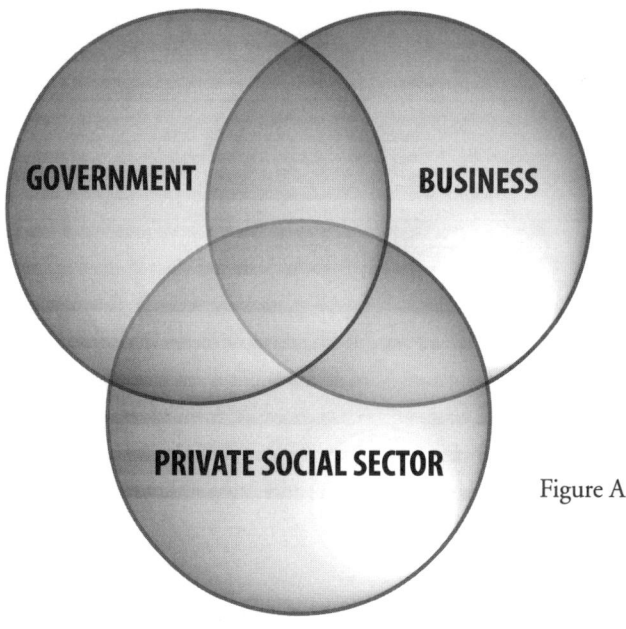

Figure A

TRANSFORMING CHARITY

The activity of civil society takes place not only in the private social sector but also in all the overlapping areas (though not everything that takes place in the overlapping areas concerns civil society). There is nothing new about this diagram. People have theoretically understood its value for some time. In practice, however, multisector approaches to problem-solving and human-services delivery are generally varied, haphazard, and built ad hoc without much foresight. What is still missing in our post-welfare reform environment is a multisector strategy—or at least a number of articulated strategies that can be locally and regionally replicated. Multisector strategies would join the best of each sector and would seek to grow two-sector relationships into three-sector relationships whenever the absent sector's contribution would help.

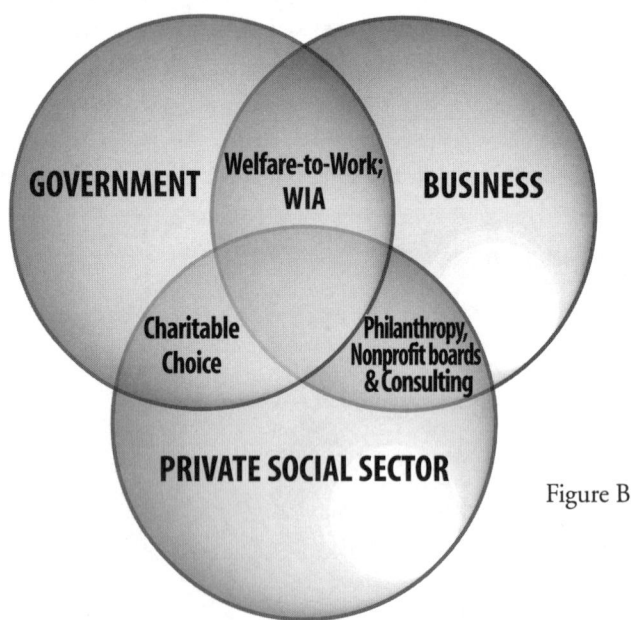

Figure B

The 1998 federal Workforce Investment Act (WIA) is an example of two-sector collaboration where government and business overlap. In its design and intent, this legislation was crafted to make the business sector at the local level a more engaged player in helping low-skilled workers integrate into the workplace. In reality, it is most successful in localities where public officials have worked hard to educate and equip the business community for its new role. In many other places, public officials maintain the old control over job training, which they enjoyed before WIA, by bewildering businesspeople with government acronyms, lengthy processes, and unhelpful program evaluations. That is, an effective two-sector collaboration is one in which each sector brings its best to the table. In this case, government functions best as a coordinator of activity and a supplier of resources, while business leaders supply their job networks and management expertise. When this works well, low-income individuals receive much better help than under the previous, government-dominated job-training programs.

The more all three sectors can play a productive role in any social issue, however, the better. Charitable Choice, for instance, is a government-nonprofit collaborative device. That is, it allows federal funds to flow through state agencies to faith-based nonprofits. As local governments use Charitable Choice, they would do well to involve the business sector in their deliberations in a serious and coordinated way. This same exercise could be practiced on a number of social welfare questions that involve multiple sectors. The future success of social welfare reform and efficacy will rest upon the degree to which this tool, or a similar one, is used to guide policy design and program implementation.

The design of a multisector strategy represents the possibility of a new civic infrastructure that, if in place, would better serve low-income and at-risk individuals by treating their predicament with full respect for its social and personal, as well as economic, complexity. No one sector can address all of the complex needs people have. Yet, recent history, and many of our current practices, ignore this point. Welfare before its reform in the 1990s made the colossal mistake of creating government systems to deal with poverty only as an economic issue, or more precisely, as a social problem that well-funded programs and well-subsidized poor Americans could overcome. Liberal academics and public intellectuals such Theodore Lowi and Daniel Patrick Moynihan recognized this already in the 1960s, but their voices were little heard, or even disregarded, by their policy-making colleagues.[14] Redistribution of income became the flimsy creed of social justice. It ignored the need for habit-transforming institutions such as churches to be fully engaged in the effort and the responsibility of businesses to take seriously the relationship between the needs of the poor and their own workforce needs. Programs were built upon the idea that poverty is a primarily economic condition. Government's job became that of attaching dollar bills as Band-Aids to the wounds of poverty.

This systemic weakness led many policy makers to cry for the shift of social welfare responsibilities entirely to the private nonprofit sector. But this view forsakes the very vital role that government (at its respective federal, state, and local levels) does in fact play in coordinating social sector activity. The success of our future efforts to solve the root causes of poverty will depend on how well we identify the key responsibilities of each sector and how well they work together, not on the relegation of full responsibility from one sector to another. This claim may not favorably strike the ears of "civil society purists" (whether in their conservative variety, which sees the social sector only as the nonprofit sector, or their liberal variety, which sees it as a government-funded, and even government-orchestrated, sector). But the claim stands on its own for two reasons. First, our current practices suggest that anything else is wishful idealism. Each sector is currently engaged in social sector, or civil society, programs and initiatives. It would require greater effort to force those programs and initiatives into one sector than to improve the ways the sectors work together to achieve the best possible results. Second, each sector offers valuable resources and capabilities that cannot be ignored. At the local level it is nearly impossible to fully address the needs of distressed communities without a contribution from each sector. Just ask any local city official or community foundation director.

Therefore, it would be more accurate to represent the social sector in Figures A and B as the entire diagram minus the nonoverlapping government and business sections. This is primarily what is referred to as the "social sector" throughout this book.

CHAPTER ONE

This is really nothing new. It is merely a way of understanding the old idea of the public square or the joint pursuit of the common good found throughout classical and modern political texts. Was the early American town hall or parish church where residents gathered to solve problems purely a function of only one sector? Alexis de Toqueville, the French journalist who visited America in the early 1830s, is routinely invoked by civil society advocates because he memorialized in his classic, *Democracy in America*, the manner in which Americans solved problems by "forever forming associations." He said in 1835, "In every case, at the head of a great new undertaking, where in France you would find the government or in England some territorial magnate, in the United States you are sure to find an association."[15] And true this was. However, the multiplication of associations in early America cannot be easily disconnected from the activities of the local government. Americans' penchant for organizing themselves to solve problems had a local governmental side as well. In fact, in the century following America's founding, local governments were multiplying rapidly. As citizens recognized the value of local government to the American ideal of self-governance, states saw the number of counties grow substantially during the nineteenth century.[16] This all happened before the massive centralization of government power in Washington, D.C., usurped a great deal of local political authority in the twentieth century. But the abuses of a large, centralized government should not make us forget the multisector nature of civil society, or the social sector, throughout much of America's history.

The strength of the social sector is of critical importance to the twenty-first century. Peter Drucker, one of the twentieth century's most prominent management theorists and forecasters of social change, has remarked, "The right answer to the question, Who takes care of the social challenges of the knowledge society? is neither the government nor the employing organization. The answer is a separate and new social sector."[17] Political consultant, Dick Morris, has interpreted the social sector's importance for political contests: "Democrats own the public sector; Republicans own the private sector. But the voluntary sector—where the action is—is up for grabs. The party that makes the voluntary sector its own will acquire a lock on

America's conscience."[18] Drucker and Morris, unlikely bedfellows, recognize that the social sector will be "where the action is" in coming generations. The only difference between their conjectures and what I am putting forward in these pages is that I think the "social sector" includes certain aspects of the government and business communities (but never those communities alone). Those individuals and organizations which are successful in formulating a multi-sector strategy for social sector innovation will have a greater influence than anyone on the conscience of America.

Two general reasons support this conjecture. First, Americans show no sign of reducing their interest and investment in the social sector. Nonprofits are multiplying, giving and volunteering are significantly high, and multisector collaborations are on the rise. But a second reason may prove more influential over time: America's need for a continually developing workforce requires a strong social sector. One reason for this is the brute fact of the growing need for workers. Especially as baby boomers retire, workers will be in demand for quite a long time to come. The Bureau of Labor Statistics projects that more than 17 million new jobs will be created between 1994 and 2005, but as Hudson Institute's *Workforce 2020* points out, that number will grow to 47.2 million once all vacated jobs (that is, the jobs made available by retiring baby boomers) are included. And of these, about half are blue-collar and low-skill occupations. The gap in skills and education between poor Americans and the rest of the population will only become more acute as baby boomers retire, but the need for low-skilled workers will be about the same in 2005 as it was in 1994.[19]

Another reason the social sector is needed to serve the demands of America's workforce concerns the interpersonal and "soft" skills employers desire in their employees. Employers continually affirm that they are as much or more interested in employees' personal and social capabilities than their technical abilities. The Welfare-to-Work Partnership's latest Report to the President states that employers are more concerned about characteristics such as dependability and a strong work ethic than about formal education and work experience. But over half of them said that they are often reluctant to hire former welfare recipients because of an inability to provide the training in the soft skills needed to succeed at work.[20] Particularly in distressed communities, people often start with a low supply of the personal, interpersonal, and baseline technical skills that are attractive to employers who have the kinds of jobs that can lift families out of poverty. And the employers that hire them cannot possibly give them all the skills they need without a network of care, probably a multisector arrangement, backing them up. So long as it is clear that soft skills and abilities affect the bottom line, employers will have a vested interest in developing them among all their workers.[21]

American communities have the opportunity to develop long-term social sector strategies. A better integration of social purpose enterprises and market-oriented institutions is needed more than ever if, for no other reason, we are to address our workforce needs. But this affords us a new opportunity to regard fellow Americans left out of the economic mainstream as valued members within it. What seemed like a novel idea only ten years ago now shows signs of becoming a normal part of American life. "Social entrepreneurship," "innovative philanthropy," and other buzzwords may pass away, but the wake of welfare reform has given us an altered environment in which our social mission and the marketplace will lose if they do not become cooperative teammates.

Three Questions in Search of Three Answers

Three questions arise when one considers the possibility of a successful multisector strategy:

1. If we are to serve individuals well by moving them out of poverty and onto a career track (rather than subsidizing further poverty, as in the old system), how can we bring the opportunities, capacity, and energy of the market together with the habit-transforming nature of mission-oriented organizations? In other words, *where does the mission meet the market?* The cultures of

mission-oriented nonprofits and businesses are almost as different as two distinct nations. Yet, to serve the entire needs of a person in an age of transformed charity, they need like never before to understand each other and work together.

2. If all sectors within a community are to be energized to form a multi-sector strategy to help the poor, what are the best ways to coordinate, equip, and leverage the assets in a community (neighborhood groups, churches, community colleges, and so on) for maximum impact? The work of churches, synagogues and mosques changes lives. Local businesses provide career tracks. Neighborhood associations organize activity and provide training. How are these socially redeeming enterprises to be connected to the larger public effort to serve the poor in the best possible way?

3. Finally, at a higher level, what kinds of tools and services are needed that will help us attract more socially oriented investment, measure the impact of existing investment, and generate a stronger performance culture within the current social sector? Enormous amounts of capital exist in the United States (and will be growing substantially over the next generation) that can be put to charitable use but remain "undeployed" due to a lack of information, the inability to harness and measure it effectively, and the lack of mechanisms to coordinate it around specific problem areas. How do we bring greater rationality to the use of this potential social-purpose capital?

Individuals, nonprofit organizations, and in some cases, entire communities have begun to supply partial answers to these questions in the form of innovative programs and initiatives. Examples of these partial answers form the larger part of Chapters Two through Four. The opportunity these three questions present will be revisited at the end of this chapter.

CHAPTER ONE

Intentions versus Investments

Our world of transforming charity requires the social sector to be multisector as a response to new challenges in serving at-risk, low-income, and indigent populations. It also requires that the resources we commit to this work are managed in ways that achieve results.

The United States is famous worldwide for its philanthropic spirit. No other country has so active a "charitable marketplace." Taking the pulse of American generosity is a way of assessing America's concern for its own civic health. Philanthropy and charity have received a lot of press in the past few years as they have undergone changes that are just as remarkable as the changes we have witnessed in the market. The $21 billion Bill and Melinda Gates Foundation, created in 1999 out of two foundations previously begun by the Microsoft founder in just 1994 and 1997, has galloped past such twentieth-century giants as the Ford Foundation in net worth. It has become America's largest foundation. Fidelity Investments' Charitable Gift Fund, the first of several mutual fund-charity hybrids that have begun in America, has become the United States' fifth-largest charity. Between its inception in 1992 and the end of 1999, it had made more than 263,000 grants on behalf of its investors, totaling more than $1 billion. And Internet sites such as www.helping.org and www.iGive.com are contributing to the growing capacity of charity to connect itself with the world of e-commerce.

The United States has seen its greatest nonprofit growth during the 1980s and 1990s, when public funds to nonprofits decreased. Canada, likewise, is proving that there is no necessary connection between decreased government grants to nonprofits (and over half of Canada's charities are government-funded) and a decrease in charitable activity. Precisely at the time that public funding of charities has grown less certain, over 1500 new charities have been emerging annually in Canada.[22] Since 1977, the number of registered nonprofit organizations in the United States has doubled, despite decreased amounts of public funding available to them. North American confidence in the social sector does not seem to be waning.

The stuff of the social sector is the stuff of America. Charity is as much a part of American history as is democracy. Just as Americans have always labored to protect their right as individuals to participate in the political process, they have worked to change the world with their charitable dollars and volunteer hours.

But it remains to be seen what the wake of welfare reform will make of American generosity and its impact on poverty and other related social ills. Much has been made in the last decade of alleged declining levels of civic engagement in America. Americans are not as involved in influencing their communities as they once were, it has been claimed, and in an age of unequaled prosperity, many of them are getting richer while leaving too many others behind. We have grown, it seems, both disaffected and crueler.

What Does American Generosity Mean?

But in 1990, with a year-end Dow of 2633, Americans gave $122 billion, while in 1999, with a year-end Dow at 9181, Americans gave more than $190 billion to nonprofit organizations—which accounts for nearly a third of all nonprofit revenue and 2.1 percent of America's gross domestic product (GDP). Three-quarters of this total came from individuals, whose giving accounts for most of the increase in giving since 1998. Giving to human-services nonprofit organizations, which account for approximately one-third of all nonprofits, was up nearly 8 percent from 1998 and 27 percent the year before. And the trend in bequest giving continues to rise, growing 14.6 percent in 1999 to reach $15.61 billion—a significant development even if the most conservative estimates are assumed about the coming intergenerational transfers of wealth. John Havens and Paul Schervish estimate in a Boston College study that at least $6 trillion of this wealth transfer will go to charitable purposes, though the number could easily grow to two or three times that amount.[23] And John Walters, publisher of *Philanthropy*, estimates that foundation assets alone may easily grow to between $4 trillion and $5.9 trillion by 2035.[24] Government spending on non-health-related social services, excluding Social Security and other pension and disability funds, exceeds $300 billion. When health services and pensions are included, the figure jumps to more than $1.5 trillion. All of the nation's federally funded highway planning and construction projects

CHAPTER ONE

account for only 73 percent of what we spend on just welfare and food stamps payments alone.[25] Altogether, America has over one million nonprofit organizations—a number up 60 percent from twenty years ago—which account for more than 6 percent of GDP and employ more than 6 percent of the American workforce.

Value of Volunteers (total value of volunteer time) 1987-1998
In billions of current dollars

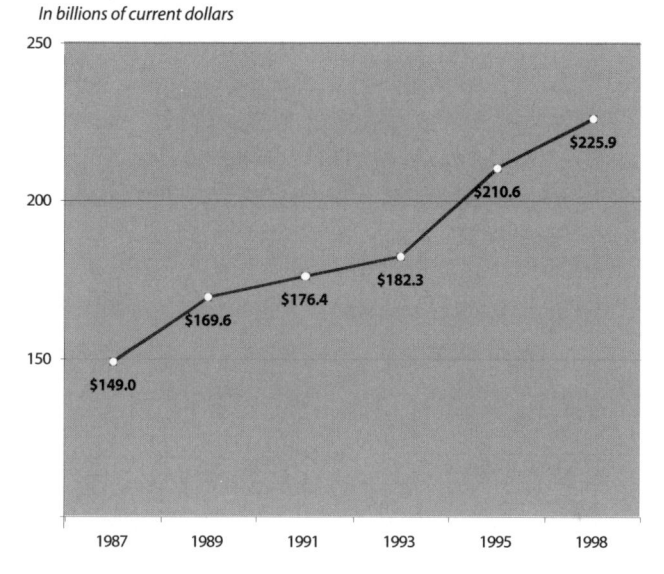

- 1987: $149.0
- 1989: $169.6
- 1991: $176.4
- 1993: $182.3
- 1995: $210.6
- 1998: $225.9

Figure C
Source: Independent Sector, 1999.

Americans have also been increasingly generous with their volunteer time. According to Independent Sector estimates, Americans volunteered nearly 20 billion hours to nonprofit organizations in 1998. More of these hours were spent on direct-service provision activity (as opposed to administrative and other overhead-related tasks) than any other single activity type. As a total, American volunteer hours represented an estimated value of almost $226 billion (see Figure C), up from $149 billion in 1987, and the equivalent of 9.3 million full-time employees.[26]

TRANSFORMING CHARITY

New Charity in the United States

Most of what has been receiving attention as "what's new" in philanthropy and social sector spending, however, is based upon what I call intention-based charity. Many individuals give on impulse to causes they believe in, even if they are quite unfamiliar with the abilities of the organizations to which they give. "One-click" Internet philanthropy—which provides Web surfers with the ability to donate directly online to a charity—may be a promising new source of dollars, but it provides perhaps the thinnest connection between donor and recipient the world has ever seen. Public spending on nonprofit organizations and for social sector problems is often done without a clear set of criteria for what constitutes a result, let alone a viable, full-blown notion of success. We remain quite content reading the anecdotes of "success" in the annual reports of charitable and public organizations, and thereby remain relatively oblivious to the actual outcomes of social sector programs. Intention-based charity is still the dominant practice in America.

Increasingly, however, today's charity is being expected to give an account not of the internal motivation it evokes in donors but of the external results. This expectation is based on a prevailing sentiment articulated by a rabbi who recently said, "A good deed is significant unto itself. Whether done for the right reason or wrong reason, the main thing is that it is actually done."[27] This sentiment increasingly expects that charity will not merely deliver goods and services to recipients but also create a greater capacity to work, advance, and contribute to the common good among those recipients. This, in turn, has required that charitable organizations and government social services build up their own capacity to create results. This may be one of the most significant, and yet underappreciated, social trends of the late twentieth century. As I have already argued, charity—understood broadly to indicate the practice of giving time and money to help the less fortunate—is in a process of transformation. With respect to the way that we manage and allocate our charitable resources, many philanthropists and other donors are increasingly wanting to move away from an intention-based to an investment-based way of doing things, even if their current practices do not fully reflect this desire.

CHAPTER ONE

A current example of a investment-oriented philanthropist stuck in an intention-based world appeared in the May 1, 2000, cover story of *Forbes*. The article featured Pierre Omidyar, the thirty-two-year-old billionaire founder of eBay, who has begun to engage in philanthropy and is strategizing how to most effectively use his abundant resources for good. The article says that "Omidyar's generation questions the efficacy of old-style charity. Walter Annenberg put up $500 million to help fight illiteracy and fund schools, but are scores up significantly? Ted Turner pledged $1 billion to the United Nations—now, there's a place that delivers value for money." And yet, the article points out that Omidyar's philanthropic "agenda is somewhat evanescent" and is focused upon rebuilding "a sense of community in America." Omidyar sees that great numbers of social problems find their roots in the way people are disconnected from one another. He is circumspect about his lack of direction on this point, but he remarks that instead of doing such things as feeding children, "We're hoping to build something that gets more children fed through second-order effects."[28] Omidyar reflects a growing sentiment that giving to a cause, however worthy, is less responsible than investing in results.

Figure D

Intention-Based Charity	**Investment-Based Charity**
"Giving and forgetting": giving resources with little or no regard for what they produce or what they are expended upon	"Giving and tracking": giving resources and then accounting for the results
Giving that relieves the immediate effects of poverty and other unfavorable conditions	Giving that addresses root causes of poverty and other unfavorable conditions
Focusing on "worthy causes": giving to an organization whose cause is honorable	Focusing on performance: giving to an organization that demonstrates the ability to produce results

39

TRANSFORMING CHARITY

As Figure D shows, the newly emerging investment-based view of charity holds that results are more important than worthy causes, and that one way to produce results is to go after the causes of problems rather than their more immediate effects. To invest in social change is to invest in mentoring relationships rather than more programs that give at-risk youth "something to do." It is to create work-based, rather than welfare-based, safety nets that help people gain the abilities to advance out of poverty rather than continue to receive cash payments. It is to invest in the creation of "social capital"—those (primarily local) networks of norms, opportunity-creating relationships, and active civic groups—that helps eliminate the causes of poverty in an individual's life and in his or her social arrangements. In short, it is to invest in the creation of relationships, support networks, and opportunity rather than well-intentioned programs alone.

What is more difficult than identifying investment-based charity is the task of accounting for how much American generosity actually qualifies as this sort. How engaged, really, are Americans in building the social capital needed to provide networks of care, opportunity, and social norms that will help eliminate root causes of poverty? No body of research exists to identify how many philanthropic dollars are investment-based rather than intention-based, because the distinction between these two kinds of giving is rarely made. And disagreement over data regarding American civic participation continues to render interpretations of that data inconclusive, which means that it will continue to be difficult to assess how "much" social capital there is in America.[29]

However, it is more important to focus on the deeper, underlying agreement in these disagreements that creating social capital is not only valuable but an important policy agenda. First theoretically articulated by James Coleman in the 1980s and later popularized in Robert Putnam's work, social capital has come to signify a vital element in a healthy society.[30] The greater one's interest and involvement in improving the well-being of his or her community, the greater the probability that the root causes of social distress in that community will be eliminated. The fact that community leaders, policy makers, academics, and public officials have begun to agree on this point is significant for the future of public policy, foundation investment, and private philanthropy.

Beyond Bickering about Social Capital

Arguments over the "level" of American generosity, which have characterized the debate over social capital in America, are less interesting than the new potential that is emerging for leveraging American generosity. How much do giving amounts and volunteer hours say about the degree to which Americans are charitable? Not enough. More important is that which today's most effective charitable groups and individuals are demanding of charity as a whole: that it focus on producing results through its generosity. Put simply, that Americans give is not as important as what that giving produces.

It is precisely this trend that creates the framework for this book. Americans are undergoing a change in what they expect of public and private resources that are distributed to reduce poverty and minimize its root causes. While still a nascent trend, there are signs of a new intentionality in the use of "social dollars." Not only are individuals and foundations beginning to think more seriously about changing the focus of charitable activity from intention-based to investment-based models, but government agencies are changing their focus from relieving the effects of poverty to transforming poverty-prolonging habits. That is, we are seeing a shift from programs that create consumers of entitlements to initiatives that encourage citizenship—defined at least in economic terms as the payment of taxes through self-sustaining employment and hopefully, as the contribution to the good of one's community.

An example of how this trend has reached government agencies can be found in the U.S. General Accounting Office's (GAO's) definition of government investment. In general, the GAO states, investment is "specifically intended to enhance the private sector's long-term productivity."[31] Included in this definition is investment in services that develop human capital, such as education and training—services that, in fact, lead the list of the GAO's estimated federal investment outlays in total dollars.[32] As the

41

GAO indicates, however, government accounting does not currently have the capability to easily distinguish between investment and noninvestment spending. The report reflects the general state of investment's relation to the social sector, and it points to the growing need for ways of measuring the efficacy and impact of social investments. But it also points to a growing dissatisfaction with current methods of accounting for the way we pay for social programs. Americans are beginning to believe that money spent on social programs should result not in the ongoing-and increasing-subsidization of social problems but in the diminishment of their causes. We might say that there is a growing belief that our social service spending should "enhance the private [social] sector's long-term productivity." Social services, it is often argued, should provide the skills and opportunities for people to leave poverty and advance in society. Investment in social services should create social capital, not inhibit its creation.

Ever since Robert Putnam published his "Bowling Alone" essay in 1995, which purported that Americans are less involved in civic organizations than they traditionally have been, academics and policy professionals have been enamored with the term "social capital." Where social capital is high, its advocates argue, people fare better economically, emotionally, and socially. The trouble in the social capital debate has been how to measure or indicate levels of social capital, which has spawned disagreements. These disagreements are almost always rooted in different interpretations of voluntary associations, and the debate has often become a sophisticated exercise in counting voluntary organizations that exist in some time and place and counting their members.[33] There is an underlying assumption that a necessary connection exists between the numbers of voluntary associations and the amounts of social capital in a community. This assumption is correct, but it is woefully inadequate in explaining social capital. Social capital is primarily about networks that create opportunity, instill civic virtues, and provide a sense of community—and voluntary organizations are certainly one of the best ways to generate these networks. However, the existence of voluntary associations does not always guarantee the creation of networks that foster social capital.

CHAPTER ONE

This book suggests that the transformation of charity offers something social capital enthusiasts may be looking for. There is little disagreement about the value of those networks of associations and norms that "social capital" indicates. But while the debate is quite advanced—even if marked by a lack of consensus—about the state of social capital, *the conversation about how to create more of it is still only in embryonic form.* This book is essentially about the generation of social capital, albeit restricted mainly to its creation in low-income communities. The transformation of charity, if carefully attended to, may result in the transformation from an era of moderate levels of social capital to an age of unprecedented social capital creation. But this will not happen if we do not begin thinking anew about how we can change our intention-based practices to investment-based strategies.

This shift from intention-based to investment-based charity is an outworking of a complex set of forces, which have been driven primarily by a changing conception of the role of government and a blurring of the lines between "the market" and "the social sector." Confidence in the ability of public agencies to deliver social services has taken a backseat to its ability to provide resources and coordinate the delivery of services by alternative providers. The welfare reform act of 1996 recognized this when it gave states complete control over moving people off welfare and into work (knowing fully well that states did not have the capacity to handle service delivery by themselves without substantial participation of the private sector). The Workforce Investment Act is a public confession that public agencies are no longer the best mechanism for designing and managing the delivery of services to the underemployed.

Tight labor markets—which, as indicated earlier, will be around for a while—have forced employers to take seriously the employee base represented by former welfare recipients and low-income individuals. This, in turn, has required employers to learn about what investing in low-skilled workers means. Helping people develop personal, or soft, skills is now as important as developing hard skills, which has required employers to begin looking to the social sector for help. At the same time, market pressures on social service agencies have made them turn to the business community in new ways for assistance in fulfilling their respective missions. "Social sector," as a result, no longer simply refers to nonprofit organizations. With the market's penetration of the social sector has come a new emphasis on results in the social sector, for better or worse. Universities are focusing more upon research in the nonprofit sector, which has resulted in the consideration of nonprofit organizations in terms of what they produce, how they are managed, and their degree of effectiveness.

In sum, the transformation of charity is one in which investments in the social sector are expected to create value. How value is created in this complex sector will be discussed at greater length in Chapter Four. For starters, though, we can safely say that in so far as individuals and families receive public assistance in its various forms (welfare-to-work payments, food stamps, earned income tax credits, housing vouchers, and so on) or create other publicly financed costs (criminal and substance abuse costs, for instance), value is created when they leave public assistance and eventually begin to contribute to the creation of financial and social capital in their communities. And, of course, they experience the creation of value in their personal lives as their standards of living and well-being increase.

Three Important Domains

It is time to begin assessing "social capital," "civic engagement," and other buzzwords of civil society enthusiasts in terms of created value rather than raw numbers of voluntary organizations or levels of civic participation alone. Considered especially in its relation to helping the poor, social capital is not of much use any other way.

This book focuses upon three domains in which today's changing charitable landscape is encouraging an investment-based approach to relieving poverty that creates social capital and builds a more civil society at the same time. These domains flow from the three questions presented earlier under the heading "Three Questions in Search of Three Answers." And, respectively, they represent the subject matter of Chapters Two through Four.

These three domains do not exhaust the possibilities for value creation, but any approach to creating value in a world of new, or transformed, charity cannot ignore them. They represent the areas of action needed to generate a more productive and coherent multisector strategy for solving social problems than we have at present. They represent the possibility of developing a new civic infrastructure without which other specific policy changes will be less effective. This book is not about specific policies relating to areas such as child care, transportation, wage laws, and other issues of great importance to low-income individuals. The civic infrastructure that could result from serious thinking about these domains would be the bedrock on which such policies would rise or fall in individual communities. These domains are as follows:

Creating new opportunities and new sources of independence. Chapter Two examines three innovative examples of connecting mission-oriented, socially redeeming nonprofit organizations to the marketplace. Each is unique in its demonstration of the way that "the mission meets the market" when imagination and concern for the poor go hand in hand. More energy is being spent today than ever on figuring out how charitable organizations can help make their clients self-sufficient, and no such organization is successful if it ignores realities such as employment training and local job market possibilities. To treat someone as a whole person is to serve his or her economic as well as emotional and spiritual conditions. Partnerships such as those discussed in Chapter Two are the key to creating new organizational entities that are not entirely social or economic. They create new sources of independence for those who need the most help becoming independent.

Creating better help closer to home by leveraging community resources. One problem faced by public agencies and foundations in their efforts to work with community-based organizations is that such efforts lack a "center." Churches, neighborhood groups, and other organizations doing great work usually operate in isolation from each other. Coordinating their efforts is a challenge, especially when it is a government office that tries to become the center of coordination. And yet communities know that they cannot improve distressed communities without them. Chapter Three concentrates on the role of intermediary organizations, which "sit" between government agencies and community groups, as an avenue for mobilizing community resources around common problems. These organizations often speak both the language of government and the language of the community. They also provide a buffer between the domains of government and religion. As government officials and community leaders increasingly recognize that their interests to improve their communities overlap (for example, both want to see reductions in teen pregnancy and improvements in the economic condition of the poor, though perhaps for different reasons), they will be confronted in an ever-increasing manner with the challenge of working in a coordinated way. How well communities engage intermediary organizations in this common effort will largely determine how well they solve their problems.

Creating new ways of assessing the results of our social investments. From newfound interest among businesses in solving social problems to emerging tools for measuring social investment's impact, we are seeing sketches of a new future for charitable practices. This future will focus upon new ways of measuring the value of social investments, which in turn will arm social-purpose organizations with the ability to demonstrate their level of effectiveness—which in turn will attract new investment, much as in the case of a business. New standards will be created, which will also enhance competition and cut down on waste. Chapter Four looks at a couple of metrics for assessing the value created when individuals move from dependency to independence. While some low-performing nonprofits and government agencies may have reason to fear what such metrics might reveal about their organizations, the populations they serve will in the long run be helped through increased accountability among service providers. This entire process assumes that we can find the right socioeconomic indicators to measure, the right standards to uphold, and the right kind of technology to coordinate and track them. Wall Street has its indicators. The social sector now needs its own.

As previously stated, the following chapters are not meant to give complete pictures of these three domains of activity. The answers to the three questions posed in "Three Questions in Search of Three Answers" are bigger than what follows. Chapters Two through Four focus on organizations and practices without which services to poor and at-risk populations would be far worse. They also represent ways in which social capital is built through the two main topics discussed in the present chapter: effective multi-sector collaborations and investment-based charity.

TRANSFORMING CHARITY

Endnotes

1 Timothy Fehler's excellent book *Poor Relief and Protestantism: The Evolution of Social Welfare in Sixteenth-Century Emden* (Aldershot: Ashgate, 1999) has served as a valuable resource on Emden's social welfare reform for this chapter.
2 Fehler, 13.
3 Quoted in Fehler, 13.
4 *The Changing Shape of the Nation's Income Distribution: 1947-1998* (Washington, D.C.: U.S. Census Bureau), 10.
5 Christine Letts, William Ryan, and Allen Grossman, *High Performance Nonprofit Organizations: Managing Upstream for Greater Impact* (New York: John Wiley & Sons, 1999), 16-19. For a more concentrated treatment of the way in which the current competitive climate in the social sector is changing what is expected of nonprofits, see Ryan's "The New Landscape for Nonprofits," *Harvard Business Review* (January-February 1999), 127-136.
6 Quoted in *USA Today*, September 23, 1999.
7 "Creating Waves in the Nonprofit Sea," *New York Times*, February 2, 2000.
8 *Change in TANF Caseloads Since Enactment of the New Welfare Law*, U.S. Department of Health and Human Services.
9 This is not to suggest it is not being done anywhere. The State of Illinois, for instance, has designed performance standards for its human services based upon keeping people in work and advancing them in careers so as to prevent the need for a return to public assistance.
10 The Census Bureau reports that the 1999 poverty rate for African Americans, 23.5, is the lowest it has ever recorded, and that the 1999 poverty rates for non-Hispanic whites and Hispanics equaled their all-time lows.
11 Robert Nisbet, *The Quest for Community* (Oxford: Oxford University Press, 1953), and Peter Berger and Richard John Neuhaus, *To Empower People* Twentieth Anniversary Edition, ed. Michael Novak (Washington, D.C.: AEI Press, 1996).
12 These data are discussed at greater length in Chapter Three.
13 IDA legislation has been passed in over half of America's states, and a number of IDA initiatives exist in others (*IDA Policy in the States*, Center for Social Development, Washington University, March 2000). Federal IDA legislation has been proposed in both houses of Congress in the Savings for Working Families Act of 2000, and again in the Senate in the American Community Renewal and New Markets Empowerment Act.
14 See, for instance, Theodore Lowi, *The End of Liberalism*, 2nd Edition (New York: Norton, 1979), and Daniel Patrick Moynihan, *Maximum Feasible*

CHAPTER ONE

Misunderstanding: Community Action in the War on Poverty (New York: Free Press, 1969). Moynihan, for one, saw through the liberal confidence in what he described as the idea that by controlling "certain inputs" into government programs, "mass behavioral change" would follow (p. 191).

15 *Democracy in America*, trans. George Lawrence (New York: HarperCollins, 1988), 513.
16 Martha Derthick writes that, for example, the number of counties grew between the Revolution and the early twentieth century "from 12 to 61 in New York, 12 to 67 in Pennsylvania, 34 to 97 in North Carolina, and 8 to 146 in Georgia. Americans had come to treat counties, even, as institutions of local self-government (and entitled as such to representation in state legislatures), rather than as administrative subdivisions of the state, serving the convenience of the state governments." Martha Derthick, "How Many Communities," in *Dilemmas of Scale in America's Federal Democracy*, ed. Martha Derthick (Washington, D.C.: Woodrow Wilson Center Press & Cambridge University Press, 1999), 129.
17 Peter Drucker, "The Age of Social Transformation," *The Atlantic Monthly* (November 1994).
18 Quoted in Don Eberly, "Compassionate Conservatism: Voluntary Associations and the Remoralization of America," The Civil Society Project, vol. 2000, no. 1.
19 Richard Judy and Carol D'Amico, *Workforce 2020: Work and Workers in the 21st Century* (Indianapolis: Hudson Institute, 1997), 71-73.
20 *The Bottom Line for Better Lives: A Report to the President on Welfare-to-Work*, The Welfare-to-Work Partnership (October 2000), 11-12.
21 Research, for instance, by The Gallup Organization shows a positive correlation between employee perceptions of the company for which they work and that company's economic performance. See Curt Coffman and Jim Harter, "A Hard Look at Soft Numbers," Liking Attitudes to Outcomes, March 1999, The Gallup Organization, and Jim Harter, "The Linkage of Employee Perceptions to Outcomes in a Retail Environment-Cause and Effect?" *The Gallup Research Journal* (Winter-Spring 2000), 25-38.
22 "Philanthropy Grapples with Competition," *Toronto Star*, November 27, 1999.
23 For the most recent statistics on giving in America, see *Giving USA* (New York: AAFRC Trust for Philanthropy). Havens and Schervish of the Social Welfare Research Institute (SWRI) at Boston College have published their research method and estimates in *Millionaires and that Millenium: New Estimates of the Forthcoming Wealth Transfer and the Prospects for a Golden Age of Philanthropy* (Boston: SWRI, October 1999).

24 John P. Walters, "Come the Revolution," *Philanthropy* (July-August, 1999), 25-26.
25 U.S. Census Bureau, *Statistical Abstract of the United States*, 1999.
26 *Giving and Volunteering in the United States: Findings from a National Survey* (Independent Sector, 1999).
27 Rabbi Benny Zippel, *Salt Lake Tribune*, May 5, 2000.
28 Quentin Hardy, "The Radical Philanthropist," *Forbes* (May 1, 2000), 116, 117.
29 Robert Putnam has famously argued that Americans' civic participation has been in decline, while Everett C. Ladd has argued the opposite. For Putnam, see "Bowling Alone: American's Declining Social Capital," *Journal of Democracy* 6 (January 1995), 65-78, and "The Strange Disappearance of Civic America," *The American Prospect* 24 (Winter 1996). He has recently published *Bowling Alone: The Collapse and Revival of American Community* (New York: Simon & Schuster, 2000). For Everett C. Ladd, who contests Putnam's conclusions, see "Civic Participation and American Democracy: The Data Just Don't Show Erosion of America's 'Social Capital'," *Public Perspective* 7 (June 1996), 1.
30 See James Coleman, "Social Capital in the Creation of Human Capital," *American Journal of Sociology* (Supplement) 94 (1988), 95-120.
31 *Budget Trends: Federal Investment Outlays, Fiscal Years 1981-2003* (GAO: June 1998), 3-4.
32 Federal investment outlays in education, training, employment, and social services-considered together-are greater than those in transportation, health, general science and space technology, environment, defense, and energy, in that order (*ibid.*, 13-14).
33 See, for instance, various essays in *Civic Engagement in American Democracy*, eds. Theda Skocpol and Morris Fiorina (Washington, D.C.: 1999). One serious attempt to measure social capital by using a complex set of variables can be found in Joshua Galper, "An Exploration of Social Capital, Giving and Volunteering at the United States' County Level," Working Paper (Urban Institute, 1999).

CHAPTER TWO
Where the Mission Meets the Market

Commercialization of social-sector organizations promises to be a fertile field for investigation far into the future, raising important theoretical questions for interested academics, and promising practical insights to social enterprise managers looking to cope with the financial strains of doing more with less.[1]

Blurring the Lines between Social and Commercial

This chapter examines three cases in which local socially redeeming nonprofit organizations (NPOs) are effectively combining their mission to at-risk and low-income families with increased market sensibilities. Together, they represent a continuum of market engagement consisting of several strategies—from a community partnership with employers to full-scale participation in the competitive marketplace.

In today's world of transforming charity, the lines between the marketplace and mission field are blurred. The institutions of charity and the market have mainly functioned independently from one another throughout the twentieth century. While corporations have made charities the objects of their philanthropic activity, few of them, until recently, have directly made equipping the poor for self-reliance a fundamental mission. And in a number of cases, foundations established by corporate entrepreneurs have favored philanthropic initiatives that fly in the face of market principles. Henry Ford II said his belief that the modern foundation is a "creature of capitalism . . . would be shocking to many professional staff people in the field of philanthropy."

But as discussed in Chapter One, the need for workers has led employers to take seriously the potential workforce that exists in low-income populations they formerly thought outside the scope of their recruitment networks. Likewise, many charities have learned that if they are to offer holistic service to the poor, ignoring the vocational needs of their clients works against their other efforts to serve personal, emotional, and spiritual needs. And some foundations and public agencies have realized that achieving social good in the form of increased self-sufficiency among families in need requires the application of business principles to their organizations and closer relationships with employers. In short, recent history has brought the mission and the market together. The market has provided a broader arena in which to achieve social purposes.

More than a fad based on an exaggerated confidence in a strong economy, the move of many nonprofits to be more market-savvy is driven by real forces. Government subsidies to nonprofits are less certain than in recent history, and private giving—while continuing to rise—is incapable of financing the entire nonprofit sector by itself. At the same time, because the number of NPOs has grown by 100 percent since 1977, competition for funds is growing more fierce.[2] Referring to this dilemma, social enterprise expert Gregory Dees, with Jaan Elias, writes, "This weakness in government and private funding, coupled with the proliferation of social sector organizations, has fueled intense competition. Accordingly, many social sector enterprises are searching for new ways to control costs, improve effectiveness, and increase revenues."[3] Organizations that not only become more businesslike in their operations but also incorporate market-based services into their overall mission are better set for the future.

As more entrepreneurial NPOs have become more market-oriented, they have begun to appear in the pages of popular and academic media. Recently, magazines such as *Time* and *Fast Company* have recognized the significance of NPOs by devoting feature articles to them.[4] This is largely because enterprising nonprofits are responding to a growing sense that our market economy is the chief engine of social change, and that the marketplace—if it is to give hope to every American—cannot be disconnected from a social mission to help those on the margins of economic opportunity. *National Journal,* a weekly staple for anyone keeping up with the inside details of politics, ran a cover story on the political relevance of market-based, transformed charity. The magazine's Carl Cannon writes, "Traditional nonprofits, overwhelmed with the endless needs of the growing legion of poor Americans, are shackled by their dependence on money or goods contributed by people who give only after their own needs and wants have been met. The new social entrepreneurs insist that this is an inefficient way to do good. Their model combines the best methods from two worlds: hard-headed fiscal conservatism and soft-hearted liberalism."[5]

The most promising examples of socially redeeming NPOs today are largely those that have connected themselves to the market by providing their clients with market opportunities and increasing their own capacity to engage in the marketplace. The answer that a nonprofit manager gives to the question, "How do we best help the people we serve reach lives of independence?" will largely determine how successfully his or her organization helps low-income clients move into the mainstream of work. How will the managers of charity marry their mission with the (often harsh) market?

Mission and Market at the Individual and Organizational Levels
The mission meets the market in two domains. The first is at the level of the individual, where people formerly regarded as "objects of charity" are regarded rather as possible players in the marketplace and thus in need of skills and opportunity, similar to the situation in sixteenth-century Emden described in Chapter One. Many organizations, including public agencies, have begun to understand their missions not as the relief of the immediate effects of poverty (hunger, shelter, insufficient resources) but as the equipping of people to overcome poverty through the cultivation of the skills and abilities that foster independence. And many organizations that have been historically preoccupied with the moral condition of the poor, such as faith-based city missions and urban churches, have realized an old Thomas

Carlyle saying: "Our works are the mirror wherein the spirit first sees its natural lineaments. Hence the folly of that impossible precept, Know thyself; till it be translated into this partially possible one, Know what thou canst work at."[6] In other words the attempt to call people to examine their inner well-being is often quite useless if their vocational well-being is in disarray. From an economic viewpoint, the integration of more at-risk and low-income individuals into the marketplace not only reduces the cost of serving them but also adds to overall productivity, which has wider economic and social benefits. From the viewpoint of the individual, the most important factor is that he or she is on the way toward economic well-being and productive membership in his or her community.

The mission also meets the market in the domain of the mission-oriented organization. Current macro forces are pushing these organizations toward a more market-based approach to fulfilling their missions. But many of them are choosing to do so because it makes sense for the services they desire to provide their clients. For some, a market-oriented approach merely means improving the access their clients have to jobs and other market opportunities. For others, it means launching their own enterprise that provides employment for clients. This can create considerable changes to the organization. The world of deadlines and contracts is often alien to the mission-oriented world of flexibility and informality. The degree to which an organization navigates these changes may be the most important factor in the quality of its future service to clients.

In what follows, three innovative models for strengthening the ability of local, socially redeeming NPOs to use the marketplace as a primary modicum of service to their clients are examined. They are the Jobs Partnership, a church-employer collaboration based in Raleigh, North Carolina; ServiceMaster Corporation's Work Training Businesses; and Roberts Enterprise Development Fund's (REDF) investment strategy for nonprofit-run enterprises. The three models can be schematized as follows:

CHAPTER TWO

Jobs Partnership: Community Partner	ServiceMaster: Business Partner	REDF: Investor
Description: Local churches lead former welfare recipients and other job-needy individuals through faith-based employment curriculum, refer them to jobs provided by local business partners, and then maintain extended mentor relationships. Jobs Partnership is the NPO that manages this partnership.	*Description:* ServiceMaster Corporation assists homeless shelters begin landscaping, housekeeping, and other service-related businesses by training their client-employees and managing their contracts with customers. It acts as subcontractor to the shelters.	*Description:* REDF, a foundation in the San Francisco Bay area, acts as a philanthropic "venture capitalist" by providing nonprofit-run enterprises that serve homeless and other needy people with assistance in business strategy, capital, and other business-capacity enhancing services, including business analysts, M.B.A. interns, and expanded area business networks.
NPO does not directly administer the employment activity of the client.	NPOs (e.g., the homeless shelters) partially administer the employment activity of the client.	NPOs (e.g., the nonprofit-run enterprises) assume full responsibility for business administration, in close collaboration with REDF.
Client's "community of support" exists largely in the NPO–sponsored mentoring relationship, with business providing some additional support in the form of a "buddy" and is a main component of program activities.	Client's "community of support" exists in the NPO's social services programs and is a major, but not main, component of program.	Client's "community of support" exists in the NPO's social services programs and is a major, but not main, component of program.
NPO ability to transition people into the world of work is largely due to its relationship with business partners.	NPO ability to transition people into the world of work is partially due to its competent subcontractor.	NPO ability to transition people into the world of work is largely due to its own business management capacity.
Low market risk: NPO is not directly affected by any negative market effects on its business partners.	Moderate market risk: depending on the degree to which the NPO makes its enterprise central to its identity, negative market effects will destabilize its operation.	High market risk: ideally, NPO makes its market presence the center of its activity and identity, and thus negative market effects highly affect the NPO.

Figure A

Several factors make the preceding models different than conventional charitable approaches to serving the poor:

- In each case the NPOs have a vested interest in the client's job performance. In fact, client success in the marketplace is a fundamental goal of the NPO, because its services are built upon the idea that a human being is both an economic and social being who needs personal healing as well as the ability to contribute to the common good.

- Ideally, NPO success is not defined by the number of people served but rather by the number of people who have moved into or toward economic independence and thus a condition of decreased reliance on conventional charity or public assistance to meet basic needs.

- In the ServiceMaster and REDF models the NPOs' ability to help their clients succeed depends heavily on their own performance in the marketplace.

These models represent charity in the age of post-welfare reform, which is really only an older version of care dressed up for the twenty-first century. The Reformation in Europe, for instance, was a time of social welfare experimentation that placed conditions on the poor and involved merchants and other commercial institutions in the work of charity. This kind of charity found its roots in instructions delivered by St. Paul, who stated that people should provide for themselves through work so long as they are able. Rather than focus on relieving the immediate effects of poverty, the organizations involved in the models presented here focus on placing clients in the work environment and helping them develop the abilities they need to work their way toward independence.

Together, these models represent a continuum of engagement that coheres nicely with what the future will demand of the social sector. This continuum includes a community partnership, a business partnership, and an investor relationship. It is not meant to replace government services but complement them and if scaled largely enough, reduce the need for them. A successful community is one that involves public and private sector leaders to create such a continuum. Each model is a unique phenomenon and deserves attention.

Jobs Partnership

Formed in 1996 in Raleigh, North Carolina, the Jobs Partnership was hatched not as a response to a social issue or welfare reform per se, but as a way of fixing a specific, local problem. Chris Mangum, of the Raleigh-based C.C. Mangum construction firm, needed workers to keep apace with booming business. Reverend Donald McCoy, an inner-city pastor, had members of his congregation in need of work. McCoy's church had hired Mangum's company to pave its parking lot, and during the course of the project, both McCoy and Mangum became aware that each held the key to addressing the other's concern. McCoy could provide workers and Mangum could provide jobs. Mangum, representative of the affluent, white suburbs, and McCoy, representative of the low-income, black inner city, realized that the "disconnect" between their respective worlds was symptomatic of Raleigh in general. They decided they had an opportunity to remedy on a larger scale the unnecessary separation in Raleigh between inner-city residents and suburban employers.

The Jobs Partnership was formed quickly thereafter. Initially a partnership between twenty-four churches and businesses, there are today over fifty churches and fifty businesses participating in the Raleigh area. Jobs Partnership runs a 12-week, two-part course designed to cultivate both workplace skills and a moral foundation. The curriculum is faith-based, which Jobs Partnership administrators unapologetically consider essential to the success of the program. Becoming job-ready, they say, is a matter of personal transformation, and the biblically based curriculum assists the students in understanding the relationship between faith in God and the value of work. The course's two parts, "Keys to Personal and Professional

Success," and "Steps to Personal and Professional Success," are taught concurrently. The former covers such topics as striving for excellence, respecting authority, resolving conflicts, and being stewards of time and money, while the latter covers practical skills needed to succeed in interviews and advance in a career.

The partnership is structured so that churches can do what they do best—coming alongside those in need—without having to manage the day-to-day affairs of a full-scale employment training program. They provide the instruction and personal attention needed to develop habits of responsibility and basic job skills in program participants. The local Jobs Partnership office conducts initial interviews, screens applicants, coordinates the courses, and assists in job placement. The participating businesses post job openings in a common database so that the participants, with the help of church mentors and Jobs Partnership staff, can select a position that fits their vocational interests and abilities. Because of this program structure, businesses receive more than a referral; they receive an accountability relationship. Not only has their prospective employee finished a solid training program, but also he or she is surrounded by a community of support that will assist in resolving any future conflicts or concerns.

Jobs Partnership has grown into a nationally replicated organization in its relatively short life. It is now operating in twenty-three cities, ten of which have been in existence for three years or more. Together, by the end of 1999, these sites had served 1109 students in their jobs program, and 916 had graduated or were working.

Getting People to Work through a Program That Works
The Jobs Partnership office in Raleigh, North Carolina, consists of two staff members and an annual budget of $105,000. It links businesses and churches, trains mentors and volunteers, screens applicants, and assists in employment placement. Since 1996, more than two hundred mentors and volunteers in the participating churches have assisted Jobs Partnership students get prepared for and integrated into the workplace. The average stu-

dent has received 88 hours of assistance from the mentor and volunteer instructors by the time they have completed three months of employment.

Between its founding in 1996 and the end of 1999, the Raleigh Jobs Partnership has had 179 students participate in its program. Of these, 140 have graduated, but others have secured employment through the program without graduating. At the end of 1999, 93 percent—or 166 former students—were working. Ninety-four percent of the graduates were still employed at that time, in keeping with local job retention rates in the Raleigh area, which, at 92 percent, are above average in North Carolina.

These high retention rates are a function of reasonably favorable work conditions. Ninety-five percent of those employed through Jobs Partnership receive benefits and work regular forty-hour weeks. The wage breakdown for those who have found jobs through Jobs Partnership is as follows:

- Thirty percent are earning between $7.50 and $8.50 per hour.

- Forty percent are earning between $8.50 and $10.00 per hour.

- Thirty percent are earning between $10.00 and $15.00 per hour.

The top-earnings bracket sits squarely within the 1999 year-end median U.S. wage range in a state that ranks thirty-first in the nation in personal income levels.[7] Thus, comparatively speaking, a substantial number of Jobs Partnership graduates are faring well by national measures. And all of them are faring well by local standards. The average hourly wage for Wake County Work First (North Carolina's welfare-to-work program) clients was lower than $7.50 in 1999.

Jobs Partnership congregations are asked to make a two-year mentoring commitment to the program participant. While the pastor often assumes a considerable amount of the mentoring load, volunteers within the congregation rotate the responsibility among themselves. Mentors usually spend one to two hours per week with the participant, which over a two-year period translates into a considerable relationship. At the end of 1999, 90 percent of program graduates were regularly attending the churches in which they were mentored. They cite the benefit of a caring community and an improved personal lifestyle as reasons why they join the church. Just as recent studies show positive effects of church attendance on such important matters as juvenile crime and physical health, Jobs Partnership provides anecdotal evidence that former welfare recipients who attend religious services experience improvement in their personal lives and economic situations.[8]

There is also a significant social benefit. The Wake County Work First office operates at more than a $4.5 million budget and employs over fifty case managers and job coaches. Its caseload dropped from 5052 in February 1995, to 2221 in February 2000. Many of existing cases are child-only cases. Jobs Partnership receives no public funds for its program and leverages far more community resources in the form of volunteer assistance than its $105,000 budget and two-person staff could yield. If regarded on a cost-per-client basis, Jobs Partnership has "saved" Wake County over $250,000, conservatively estimated.

A Holistic Program

The distinctiveness of the Jobs Partnership model is in its breadth of service and its holistic treatment of program participants. Vicky Church, program director for community partnerships in the North Carolina Department of Social Services, articulates five points that set Jobs Partnership apart from other vocational programs:

1. *Trained, long-term mentoring.* A two-year commitment to mentoring is substantial, if not extraordinary. The fact that mentors are not only trained but also present during the student's job-training exercises creates an atmosphere for the building of trust and mutual respect that exceeds normal mentoring-based programs.

2. *Solid, values-based job training.* The biblically based employment training curriculum reinforces many of the values held in common in North Carolina, such as respect for authority and an understanding that work is a vital part of a person's overall spiritual, emotional, and physical well-being.

3. *Job database system.* Over four hundred jobs are posted in Raleigh alone at any given time in the Job Partnership's central database. Businesses not formally associated with Jobs Partnership regularly request permission to post their jobs there as well, due to their respect for the program and the quality of its graduates.

4. *Follow-up system.* Before North Carolina laws changed permitting Department of Social Services caseworkers to follow up with clients for a period longer than three months after job placement, the Jobs Partnership was already practicing a long-term follow-up strategy. Because students are placed in jobs well before the first of the two mentoring years is completed, the mentoring relationship continues for an extensive time period.

5. *Workplace buddy system.* Jobs Partnership's required buddy system at the student's place of employment not only gives increased personal attention beyond the church-based mentor but also provides another resource for problem-solving. While the regular mentor is expected to make interventions in personal—sometimes even serious—matters, the buddy can help the employed student resolve workplace conflicts as well as arrange solutions to transportation and other work-related problems.

While other programs incorporate one or two of these elements into their programs, Church claims, Jobs Partnership is the only organization in North Carolina to have successfully combined them into a single package.[9]

TRANSFORMING CHARITY

Jobs Partnership represents a new entity created in an intentional community partnership. Churches expand their mission. Businesses receive well-equipped entry-level employees. And former welfare recipients find a new community of support. The partnership embodies lessons that have applicability to other programs and organizations.

1. Because people do not separate their vocational from their spiritual selves, they are best served by programs that address the "whole person": the partnership unabashedly makes the road to work concurrent with spiritual development, to which no significant protests have been raised by participants.

2. The wall that often exists between business and the faith community does not have to exist: Jobs Partnership represents one way in which these two fundamental sets of institutions can create a larger community of cooperation.

3. Technology can be a unifying mechanism: though quite simple, the jobs database provides a central coordination component.

4. The creation of an independent nonprofit—in this case, Jobs Partnership—to coordinate and manage the effort creates a coherence that might otherwise be lacking if the churches and businesses attempted to work together in a looser, decentralized partnership.

Jobs Partnership has attracted much attention nationwide for the way it has brought together the business and faith communities to cooperate in an unprecedented manner to solve a tough problem. What began as a pragmatic answer to local problem is now the stuff of leading practices. But the story would be incomplete, according to Chris Mangum, if what is perhaps the most important phenomenon were left out.

> *"Through the Jobs Partnership," he explains, "the minority church has been put in a leadership role in the program where power is truly transferred from the traditionally powerful—in this case, the affluent business community—to the traditionally weak, the minority church. In my opinion, it is this power transfer that is responsible for the aggressive ownership of the program we see among the participating churches."*

Mangum also points out that largely white businesspeople and largely black clergy and inner-city residents are building relationships in ways like never before. They show up at each others' homes for cookouts, get their families together, engage in prayer together. What began as a jobs program has grown into an engine of racial and economic reconciliation. Jobs Partnership consultant James White says,

> *"Efforts at racial integration have usually been a form of cheap assimilation in which blacks work to 'fit into' larger society without experiencing any real empowerment in the process. The Jobs Partnership is a model in which power is equally distributed, in which the affluent learn to give it away, in which the pastors that have not had much of it in the past learn how to use it appropriately."*

ServiceMaster's Work Training Businesses

Social purpose organizations that engage in commercial enterprise have grown in popularity in recent years. Some mainstays such as Goodwill Industries, which has revenues of $1.65 billion, nearly $800 million of which comes from its merchandise resale businesses and 84.3 percent of which is spent on its human services programs, have long been engaged in "mixing mission and market." But it has been in the past two decades that we have seen a greater proliferation of such organizations than was previously the case. Seattle-based Pioneer Human Services, a well-known enterprise that employs former prisoners and recovering addicts in a $50 million business portfolio, is an example of how commercial strategies can change an organization. Pioneer began its market focus in 1984, when it was a $4 million organization that received three-quarters of its funding from government grants. Such stories inspire others, but they are rare because ventures such as Pioneer are both relatively new and often difficult to make work.

A commercial focus in a nonprofit, mission-oriented environment brings with it both great possibility and great risk. An enterprising approach gives the organization a way to deliver social goods without fostering dependence in their clients—in fact, if done correctly, it should foster independence over time. But there is also increased risk due to the challenge of playing hardball in the market. With a new business failure rate of 70% in the United States, nonprofits cannot expect an easy ride in the marketplace.[10]

For this reason, nonprofits with an enterprising spirit do well to connect with a business partner that can reduce the odds of their failure. ServiceMaster Corporation is one such partner through its Work Training Businesses program, and it provides a forward-looking example of a way in which mission and market can come together to benefit all involved.

Producing Economic and Social Value

The ServiceMaster Corporation, one of the world's foremost outsourcing companies, generates annual revenues in excess of $6 billion and is active in forty-one countries. Long driven by a mission to help people develop, it started its Work Training Businesses program in 1993 with the goal of transitioning homeless and other at-risk individuals into lives of economic stability. The program is designed to help nonprofit organizations that serve poor populations create enterprises in which their program participants—called trainees—can work and develop marketable skills. The nonprofits, with ServiceMaster's assistance if needed, secure contracts from paying customers for landscaping, housekeeping, and related services. The nonprofit then outsources management services to ServiceMaster. These services include managing the business contract with the paying customer, employee training, and work-site supervision.

CHAPTER TWO

The nonprofit can thus continue to focus its valuable human resources on what it does best—namely, helping people overcome personal barriers, whether emotional or material—while having ServiceMaster administer operational essentials. And unlike many nonprofits that embark on a mission to run businesses but fail because of a lack of business acumen, those that establish a Work Training Business not only benefit from ServiceMaster's business expertise but also guarantee top-quality service to their customers.

This arrangement is not unlike a conventional business relationship in which significant services are outsourced. But because it involves a nonprofit, social purpose organization, the business entity created by this relationship is different from a conventional for-profit in two major ways, both of which have to do with how it measures success.

1. Trainees are developed not to be retained but to be transitioned into the mainstream marketplace. The program is designed to last two years per trainee, during which time the requisite skills and experience are learned. In many cases, however, trainees will prove competent enough to find work before completing the program. Whatever the case, unlike a standard for-profit business, which (at least theoretically) provides incentives to keep its best workers, these socially redeeming nonprofits strive to advance their best workers out of the Work Training Businesses program and into lives of self-sufficiency. While a small number of the trainees will eventually be promoted to supervisor level, this nevertheless creates a sizable challenge for program administrators, for whom high turnover rates are a built-in part of the program design.

2. Because the enterprise is a nonprofit, net revenue is invested back into the overall mission of the organization, which is to serve people rather than increase shareholder portfolios. These investments have returns that create social value rather than personal or corporate wealth. This social value comes from improved lives and can be measured economically both in terms of savings to taxpayers for ser-

vices no longer used and in terms of increased actual output. Social value created in this way also increases the likelihood that habits promoting independence will be transferred to children, thus reducing the likelihood that those children will become dependent on public resources or private charity.

Case Study: Chicago Christian Industrial League

The Work Training Businesses program is a relatively recent venture. In 1993 ServiceMaster launched it with the Chicago Christian Industrial League (CCIL) in Chicago by helping CCIL form a landscape business. A $7.7 million operation, CCIL has a ninety-year history of serving the homeless in Chicago. Its self-styled "holistic" approach to serving its clients includes not only room and board but also the requirement that residents participate in a range of services including job training, personal development, counseling, and educational courses. Its resident population, on average, ranges between 275 and 325 individuals, and it annually serves over 275,000 meals to more than 700 people. But it considers its hallmark to be its ability to transition more than a hundred people annually into self-sustaining employment. CCIL's mission has long been to equip its clients with skills needed to become independent, but before its landscaping venture, this translated into little more than life-skills training.

It was through CCIL's initiative that the opportunity first arose to contract with the City of Chicago to provide landscaping services. They then turned to ServiceMaster for assistance—a partnership that provided the context for the development of ServiceMaster's Work Training Businesses methodology.

CCIL's landscape business has had a twofold stated purpose.

1. To provide work opportunities for CCIL clients and help them transition to independent living—in short, the development of *human capital*

2. To develop a self-sustaining revenue stream to support the mission and operation of CCIL—in short, the development of *financial capital*

With respect to human capital, the program has provided work opportunities for 550 people since its inception. Over 65 percent have successfully moved into permanent employment or have furthered their education and training. Before enlisting ServiceMaster's help, CCIL had successfully placed 40 percent of their working clients into permanent employment or education. At the end of 1999, program graduates were earning, on average, between $8.50 and $9.00 per hour in jobs they secured upon leaving the program (they earn, on average, $7.50 per hour during the program). While these wages do not represent a livable wage for a family in Chicago, they do represent the beginning of a journey away from a far worse condition—that of homelessness, addiction, hopelessness. Significant as well is the $20 million that the Chicago Department of Human Services annually spends to serve the 10,000 people estimated to be homeless on any given day in Chicago. Programs such as CCIL's Landscape Services represent the beginnings of a potential reduction in the resources needed to serve the homeless, especially those who stand a good chance of becoming employable.

Beyond success in job placement and economic impact, the Work Training Businesses place a central focus upon leadership, technical knowledge, and skills training. From the start of the program, trainees learn the standards they are expected to meet and uphold along with the required skills for achieving the standards. They spend 10 percent of their workweek learning about horticulture, mechanical skills, and work processes. As a result of the program's disciplined approach to training, the ratio of ServiceMaster managers to CCIL trainees in the program has been reduced from one-to-three to one-to-ten between 1993 and 1999. The ratio of on-site supervisors to employees has remained constant, however, because graduates of the training program have been promoted to supervisory positions.

Serving trainees well has not come without difficulties. During the first three years of the program, successful post-program placement in employment or education was at 78 percent. Between 1995 and 1997, this number dropped to 28 percent, due in large part to the rapid growth of the program. The number of trainees and amount of business quadrupled during this time. According to Noel Jackson, CCIL's chief financial officer, by

1995, the landscaping business had won the respect and trust of its customers, which resulted in contract awards that almost overwhelmed the operation. CCIL and ServiceMaster worked diligently to develop the administrative capacity to deal with such dramatic growth, and by 1997, they had remedied the problem. They perfected their training processes and designed a master gardener program to give trainees wintertime employment and the skills to secure such post-program employment as tree specialists, salaried groundskeepers, and CCIL Landscape Services supervisors. In general, they enhanced the training and skills options for program employees and thus created a human capital development environment. The close of the 1999 season saw a 55 percent success rate in terms of those actively working or furthering their education. Of those who leave the program before completion, it is not known how many find employment.

Regarding financial capital, CCIL Landscape Services grew from $330,000 gross revenues in 1993 to $3.5 million in 1998. It has held contracts with the City of Chicago's Department of General Services and Transportation and the Chicago Public Schools. It has maintained green space in some of Chicago's most visible, highly trafficked areas and more than two hundred school properties and parks. Unlike most nonprofit job training and placement programs' reliance upon contributions and grants for revenue, CCIL Landscape Services generates a profit from its contracts, which enables it not only to be fully self-supporting but also capable of investing in related CCIL infrastructure.

Over 50 percent of CCIL's total revenue comes from its landscaping business, which employs only 13 percent of its resident population in a given year. When numbered among total people served annually by CCIL (residents and nonresidents), the trainees within the landscaping business constitute less than 25 percent of the total.[11] Thus less than 25 percent of CCIL's client base generates over half of CCIL's total revenue.

In the year before the landscaping business was formed, CCIL relied almost entirely upon conventional funding such as contributions and grants. In this traditional scenario, services to clients are costs, financially considered, and are often restricted (especially when publicly granted) to

CHAPTER TWO

certain usage. When an enterprise such as CCIL's landscaping business becomes a part of the organization, its revenue is not restricted by the kinds of conditions accompanying public and private grants, and services can now be understood in terms other than "cost." They may also be understood in terms of the value they provide the enterprise, much like human capital investments in a for-profit business.

By the end of 1999, CCIL's landscaping service helped the organization capitalize new services. An adult education program was implemented to raise client reading capabilities to the level necessary to be employable, and GED courses were offered on-site for the first time. Three full-time, on-site therapists have been hired to address the psychological needs of clients that previously went unmet. Finally, a job-readiness component has become a regular part of CCIL operations and offers clients the skills they need to be competitive in the marketplace.

One very important consequence of CCIL's pursuit of its landscaping objectives has been the degree to which it has altered its own administrative culture. According to Jackson, expectations for producing results are more clearly articulated and communicated within the administration. Begun initially as an "incomplete idea with no real business plan," the landscaping services now sets the standard within the organization for assessing progress and success.

Accountability for progress and results are a very real part of the organizational culture that, only six years earlier, had no verifiable commitment to outcomes. This is largely due to the very crude fact that producing quality work and satisfying the conditions of the paying customer demand a sense of urgency alien to most social service organizations. Bill Bedrossian, chief operating officer of ServiceMaster's Work Training Businesses, says, "Even if hiring an organization like CCIL to do work satisfies a customer's desire to do something good for society, as soon as the contract is signed, that customer will forget you are a social service agency."

The clearest demonstration of CCIL's commitment to a "work first," results-oriented culture is its approach to case management. Because a person's life is a continuum—not a collection of parts to which "services" can

69

be directed one by one—CCIL decided that their social services and work training needed greater congruence. Case managers, the organization contended, could not properly serve their clients if they did not understand the work-training process that was in itself making valuable contributions to client development. CCIL thus required their ten case managers to go to job sites, attend work-training sessions with the clients, and help the clients tailor paths to self-sufficiency in coordination with their vocational development. When the case managers refused to cooperate, CCIL terminated all of them in 1999 and replaced them with what are now called client service facilitators, whose job requires them to participate in all aspects of client development.

Capacity Building

ServiceMaster's interests in Work Training Businesses are not simply altruistic. By investing in these relationships, ServiceMaster intends to create for itself a source of trained workers from within the nonprofit enterprises, create a reasonable revenue stream from a formerly ignored market, and strengthen its business position within the broader community in which it launches its Work Training Businesses. In order to do this, however, its primary objective has been to build capacity in the NPOs with whom it works so that they are capable of long-term impact—which for them is moving people into lives of independence while generating a profit. Because the nonprofits regard work experience as the fundamental means by which they can transition their clients into self-sufficiency, capacity building is largely the task of creating a business-savvy environment within the organization. ServiceMaster's market interests are met when it helps the nonprofits accomplish their market-oriented missions.

On a smaller scale than its partnership with CCIL, ServiceMaster has replicated its Work Training Businesses program in Indianapolis and South Bend, Indiana, and in DuPage County, Illinois, and is currently launching new operations in several cities across the United States. In each case ServiceMaster is faced with the task of "marrying a market with a mission," that is, of creating a socially redeeming enterprise that nevertheless navigates the market like any for-profit competitor. Because of the two distinctive features of these unique enterprises described earlier (continual turnover and the investment of profits into human services), business-minded management is essential to the success of the enterprise's overall contribution to the lives of its clients and its organization. For ServiceMaster, success in its Work Training Businesses is based not only upon its management of some component of work, as it is with its conventional clients, but also in its ability to foster administrative capacity in the nonprofit with whom it is partnering.

In Indianapolis, for example, it helped Wheeler Mission Ministries, a hundred-year-old inner-city homeless shelter and service provider, establish Wheeler Enterprises (WE). With ServiceMaster's help, WE bid on and won a $150,000 mowing contract with the City of Indianapolis in the spring of 1999 that employed one ServiceMaster manager and a crew of six trainees. This enabled WE to establish itself as a business entity in the city, and at the end of 1999, it had purchased a $300,000 window-cleaning business. Within three months, the window-cleaning business hired four trainees and one crew leader from within Wheeler's client base, and was adding new business almost weekly. Today, trainees are paid a base wage plus 10 percent of the revenue their team generates each week. Crew leaders are paid a salary plus a onetime bonus for any new business they win, scaled to the size of the contract. The window-cleaning operation's business plan projects that within eighteen months, it will generate the capital necessary to fund a rural drug rehabilitation program to serve addicts in outlying areas. Wheeler Enterprises currently employs more than twenty people, and by the end of 2000, it will be a $500,000 operation. Its revenues have covered its costs faster than expected, and its directors expect the operation to reach profitability within the first quarter of 2001. ServiceMaster's investment in building a business culture within WE has paid off.

The most concrete manifestations of capacity-building through ServiceMaster's Work Training Businesses can be summarized as follows:

1. *Increased responsibility for business operations within the nonprofit organization.* In CCIL's case, this is evidenced by the reduced percentage of ServiceMaster employees per trainee and by its reinvention of the caseworker's role. By hiring program graduates back into its Work Training Businesses as supervisors, CCIL is growing technical expertise within its organization, and by demanding that caseworkers conform to the continuum of the trainees' lives and not vice versa, CCIL collapses the gap between social services and work training. These factors help address the unique problem of "intentional turnover" inherent in the program. Technical expertise and enterprise-minded case managers are critical components to reducing the cost of base-level training, which is a continual and dominant part of a high-turnover environment.

2. *Expansion of services.* For CCIL, revenues have been used to make core human services more multidimensional by adding enhanced job training, therapy, and other personal development services. The business has also provided the capital needed to create the housekeeping training program in 1995 and the food-service training program in 1997. In 1998, with partial assistance from a foundation grant, the master gardener program was created. These three programs provide additional vocational training for nearly a hundred people annually.

The Mission, the Market, and the Future

Growing more programs such as ServiceMaster's Work Training Businesses throughout our society will depend largely on how well social purpose business managers handle the two distinguishing characteristics of such enterprises: inherent turnover and socially redeeming "profits."

Most social purpose enterprises such as CCIL Landscape Services will best deal with the first characteristic, turnover, by doing the following:

1. They will hire strong case managers familiar with the business and be able to get new hires up to speed.

2. They will implement solid recruitment strategies, which should involve relationships with public agencies as well as churches, schools, and other community organizations.

3. They will be dedicated to hiring graduates back into the program, since graduates can best relate to new hires.

4. They will cultivate good relationships with area employers, some of whom may be competitors, to whom they can refer graduates.

With respect to social investment, or the second characteristic, social purpose enterprises will need to focus upon two kinds of investment.

1. They need to evaluate—and hire strategic consultants if they are not confident in their own assessment capability—the kinds of additional services that will assist their clients to achieve independence. Making sure that all the services are well-coordinated with each other is essential for maximum impact.

2. The organization needs to invest in its own capacity to measure its clients' progress, its ability to manage relationships with donors and business clients, and its overall administrative capacity.

There are an increasing number of consultants specializing in these themes, and it is a safe bet that the next decade will see the development of a new services industry based on strengthening the social sector marketplace. This is already happening to some degree, and it will likely become more common for enterprising NPOs to solicit professional help in capacity building, capital development, and strategic planning.

The Roberts Enterprise Development Fund— a New Breed of Investor

If Jobs Partnership connects churches to the market through a partnership with the business community, and ServiceMaster through its role as a business partner, The Roberts Enterprise Development Fund (REDF) engages NPOs in the marketplace as an investor. REDF is in the business of ensuring the long-term viability of its grantees by investing in their organizational capacities in ways more akin to venture-capitalist practices than conventional foundation practices. REDF's manner of doing things is an example of what Letts, Ryan, and Grossman wrote in their widely read article, "Virtuous Capital: What Foundations Can Learn from Venture Capitalists," which advocates that foundations adopt something of an investment-based philanthropic approach. This "makes sense," they say, because "foundations and venture capitalists face similar challenges: selecting the most worthy recipients for funding, relying on young organizations to implement ideas, and being accountable to the third party whose funds they are investing."[12] Ahead of the game in this respect, REDF has become perhaps the most experimental of venture philanthropists. It outpaces others in terms of its ongoing self-analysis, and continuously documents its learning.

Creating Social Returns on Investment

The Roberts Foundation of San Francisco founded the Homeless Economic Development Fund (HEDF) in 1990 on the premise that employment opportunities rather than housing should be the primary mode of service for the homeless. This flew in the face of conventional wisdom. Community development organizations focused mainly upon creating affordable housing, and government job training dollars were largely unavailable for homeless populations.[13] This, of course, should be no surprise. Acts of charity for the homeless have long been focused upon the provision of food and shelter—the two primary needs of the homeless when viewed through the eyes of conventional charity. While provision for these basic needs are fundamental and necessary, without investment in the long-term employability of the homeless, they represent a "thin" charity that cares for the present without much thought of the future.

HEDF, based upon the conviction that the homeless are best served by preparing them for participation in the marketplace, funded organizations that increased the employability of homeless individuals. Between 1990–1996, HEDF granted more than $6 million to more than forty organizations in the Bay Area. During this time, HEDF's directors increasingly concentrated their funding on nonprofit-run enterprise creation and began to withdraw support from organizations that relied upon traditional job-training methods.

The greatest long-term impact, they discovered, was to be found in building up nonprofit-run enterprises that provided employment opportunities for the homeless while carving out niches for themselves in the marketplace. From gourmet baked goods to custom carpentry products, the Bay Area is home to some of the most innovative, socially redeeming enterprises in the nation. Unlike traditional job-training services, which generally focus on short-term training and job placement, these social purpose enterprises aim at preparing their clients for long-term employability. And the enterprises have a greater stake in the performance of their clients than the traditional service providers whose existence rarely depends upon the long-term success of their clients.

Working with social purpose enterprises taught HEDF's leadership that, first, the enterprises could in fact become active competitors in the marketplace, contrary to the opinion of many detractors, and second, success for the enterprises was largely a function of their capacity to manage, develop, and create business—a well-known weakness of the average NPO.

Perhaps the greatest lesson for HEDF was that as it became more involved in maturing the business capacity of the enterprises, it was changing its own role from that of grant-maker to that of investor. Rather than a projection of a well-formulated theory, this change came about in HEDF's practices. Instead of reviewing its clients' grant proposals, it began to craft business plans with them. Instead of funding innovative programs, it paid for business analysis and capitalized potential revenue-generating enterprises.

TRANSFORMING CHARITY

In short, it recognized that by investing its dollars in the capacity of the enterprises to carry out their business plans over time on their own, it was actually *creating* value. Value in this case is not only that of increased gross product but also the reduction in the cost of prolonged unemployment, both to the public purse and to the other private programs—not to mention to the lives of those employed by the enterprise.

In 1996 HEDF was dissolved and the Roberts Enterprise Development Fund (REDF) was established early in 1997 to pursue a full-blown venture-capital approach to funding nonprofit-run enterprises. REDF represented a full departure from the conventional philanthropic approach of most foundations. Conventional grant-making is marked by "distance" between the foundation and the recipient, low levels of risk for the foundation, and funding for programs. REDF's strategy emphasizes a close relationship with the enterprises in which it invests, shared risk in the success of the enterprises, and capital directed not at programs but at building business capacity.[14]

It is currently fashionable to assert that nonprofit organizations need improved capacity to make it in the future, but that may or may not be true depending on what one means by "capacity." REDF has an advanced understanding of capacity. Investing in their portfolio enterprises takes the following forms:

- *Core investments:* These are in the $100,000 range and are invested in the human capital needed to execute a business strategy as projected in a business plan.

- *Capital investments:* Additional capital may be invested as deemed necessary to fulfill the aims of the strategy.

- *Business analyst:* REDF employs an enterprise development director to provide ongoing expert analysis and consultation.

- *Venture committees:* Formed by members of REDF, the enterprise, and experts in the enterprise's market sector, these groups meet monthly to review performance and make adjustments.

- *Farber interns and fellows:* Whether for a summer or a year, these individuals are M.B.A. students that REDF employs to help enterprises build their businesses and gain experience in the process (that will hopefully benefit the social sector of the future).

- *Partners-for-Profit:* Composed of area business leaders, this group provides REDF's portfolio enterprises access to professional networks and expert counsel.

- *Access to technology:* REDF not only provides basic needed technological infrastructure but also is working with its portfolio to design customized databases that enable the enterprise managers to track its social impact.

- *Social return on investment:* This technology, which has been in design for several years and is now being implemented, enables enterprises to track both social and economic indicators in a sophisticated matrix that will equip enterprise managers to understand their organization's performance as fully as possible.[15]

Because REDF's strategy is new, no long-term evaluation is available to assess its overall merit. However, it is beginning to show results. The following case study is an example of what REDF's unique approach yields.

Case Study: Community Vocational Enterprises

Community Vocational Enterprises (CVE) is a fourteen-year-old nonprofit providing job training and employment for people with psychiatric disabilities in San Francisco. CVE offers a full array of services to its more than two hundred annual clients, ranging from educational to vocational to personal skills assistance. In 1991 CVE began a janitorial enterprise to provide steady in-house employment for its clients and a revenue stream for the organization. Without a business plan, CVE cobbled together $140,000 in contracts to put some of its clients to work, but it became evident after a couple of years that the business would not grow without more direct strategic attention.

CVE began working with REDF in 1996 with the hope of increasing its enterprise development, and in 1998, it launched Industrial Maintenance Engineers (IME), an extension of its janitorial business. REDF helped CVE create a detailed, nine-year business plan designed to draw in more revenue and enable CVE to self-fund the currently subsidized social services that IME employees use. The average employee of IME requires approximately $3800 of supportive services annually. As the business grows, the cost of social services is projected to decline, because the business plan is based on a phaseout strategy for the cost of these services as they are absorbed by increased revenues. It also builds in the added value of the vocational training that IME employees receive, which over time reduces the number of supportive services that they require. There are, of course, economies of scale built into the plan as well, such as the ability to train more employees at less cost as they are added, due to the relatively fixed costs of IME training.

IME is on track with its business plan to reach its June 2001 target of $650,000 of business. The plan has helped CVE identify its target markets and manage its new business. REDF's regular interaction with CVE leadership does not only install a level of accountability unknown to many nonprofits but also creates a forum in which adjustments can be made and changes navigated before a problem arises.

CVE, a $2.4 million operation, receives income from a combination of government grants, conventional foundation grants, and revenue generated from IME and several smaller enterprises such as food services and messenger service businesses. While less than half its revenue comes from enterprise revenues, it is on track—again, according to its business plan—to reverse this within a few years. Together with its regular consultation, REDF currently invests $100,000 in CVE's business development, pays for a business analyst, makes a Farber intern available, and provides additional capital for technology infrastructure, social outcome tracking, and staff capacity-building such as training and new hiring. Compared to CVE's total income, REDF's investment is small but is already creating new assets beyond added revenue: the human and knowledge capital necessary for CVE to continue to generate future revenues.

CVE is planning to use the growing IME to finance the start of a new enterprise modeled on IME's success. IME is CVE's only long-term employment option for CVE clients, and there is a need for more parallel enterprises. CVE is currently researching the market, with REDF's assistance, for its best "business match." While only in the beginning stages of creating a new enterprise, CVE's confidence comes from the success of IME. Another added benefit is experienced by IME's employees themselves. There are currently thirty-five employees. Their first year is a training tier after which they may become regular, full-time staff. Before REDF's involvement, there was not enough business to offer a diversity of scheduling and site options for prospective employees. CVE's client needs are diverse and often require employment schedules to fit within their other services needs. Some can work nights, some days. The business plan has equipped IME to secure a varied set of contracts that offer multiple scheduling opportunities, which has enabled CVE to offer employment to a broader range of clients than before the development of the plan.[16]

This story could be repeated a number of times. REDF's investment portfolio consists of more than twenty social purpose enterprises employing more than 600 individuals. Since just 1998, more than a thousand people have found employment through one of the REDF–sponsored enterprises.[17] Such a figure warrants pause for a rhetorical question: where else would these one thousand plus individuals have gone for employment? Without the capacity to both run a successful business and serve people facing significant barriers to a career, many social service organizations, unlike REDF's portfolio enterprises, are underequipped to serve the needs of their target populations.

Conclusion: What the Public Sector Should Be Doing with All of This

This chapter has focused upon three examples of social sector innovation that represent the future—or at least the best of it. Together, they help paint a picture of how the world can look where mission and market come together. They present a snapshot of how combating poverty through employment can succeed in a world where organizations are dealing with increased competition for resources and an increasing congruence between social and commercial purposes.

Ventures such as the three discussed here will likely multiply. Changes in technology and services will continue to create the framework for a performance-driven culture within nonprofit organizations. Increased accountability to funders through these changes will force nonprofits to show results, and one of the best ways to do this is to bring their conventional human services "closer" to the market so that the clients' economic, emotional, spiritual, and physical needs may be served. Traditionally, equipping clients for economic self-sufficiency has not been a central part of many of these organizations' programs. And finally, the trend toward devolution of social services will continue. Its embodiment in federal laws such as the welfare reform act push us in that direction. Information technology provides localities with expanded networks, making centralization less necessary. Communities are better equipped than ever before to solve their problems, and they have greater access than ever to leading expert counsel because of various capacity-building efforts sponsored by foundations and public agencies. New attention is being given to generating capital at the local level and in enterprising ways such that—if advanced—federal grants will eventually look more and more like an arcane way of funding development.[18]

Government the Coordinator

The most forward-looking activity at the intersection of mission and market will happen in the private sector, but public officials should recognize what this means for them. Government can help create an environment suitable for developing partnerships like those found in Jobs Partnership, ServiceMaster, and REDF in two general ways. First, it can be the coordinator, convener, and organizer of local communities to develop partnerships like these. This is largely a function of the will and imagination of local public officials. Their willingness to bring local businesses and community-based groups together is crucial. Their ability to foster a shared vision among these sectors is also crucial. Government has historically been well-positioned to link various actors in a community around a central project or set of projects. Government officials also need to be prepared to make socially redeeming partnerships palatable to businesses through innovative tax scenarios and incentive structures for for-profit and nonprofit organizations that advance people toward careers.

Government the Investor

The second general role for government is that of investor. It can invest in two ways. Before discussing these, however, a word about "government investment" is in order.

It has become fashionable to use the word *investment* while describing government funding of social programs of all kinds, but in reality, actual social investment is practically nonexistent today. Public officials and policy makers regularly talk of investing in education, job training, housing, and so on, but they are really only talking about funding—or simply, spending. For example, the Workforce Investment Act, besides using the word in its title, is stocked with investment terminology. Government officials should quit using "investment" as a metaphor for funding until they have some way of proving that "returns" are actual and demonstrable. While new efforts are underway to begin tracking government spending similar to the way one tracks an actual investment, which will be discussed in Chapter Four, current practice is still in "funding mode." In reality, governments disburse, or spend, money. Only in rhetoric are they investing.

Government investment should be understood as using resources to create value in a way that decreases future need of public resources and increases private-sector productivity. Spending does not do this. Welfare spending after the 1960s brought about a greater *consumption* of future resources. This brings us to the first way that government involvement can invest in the creation of socially redeeming enterprises and partnerships. In the spirit of its research and development investment, it can invest in the *develop-*

ment of new capacity-building tools and services that will enrich the social sector marketplace. These would include tools that measure outcomes in a more effective fashion than is currently practiced, which would in turn enable nonprofit organizations to give account for their work and adapt to unfavorable projections before it is too late. These tools would also connect donors to the results of their social investments through a reasonable form of quantification, much like investors track the results of their financial investments.

A second area of possible government investment is directly in the *creation of promising new social purpose enterprises* in particularly troubled areas. Capital could be provided at a discounted rate of return and supportive services provided to ensure that the capital achieves the intended results. Better yet, government agencies could identify—or help to create, if necessary—nongovernmental organizations such as REDF to actually do the investing. We may or may not want to consider the possibility of a Fannie Mae–style venture fund, but even if such an idea is too far-flung, a government-initiated set of social venture capitalists could help create an active industry the likes of which we have not yet seen.

CHAPTER TWO

Endnotes

1. Gregory Dees and Jaan Elias, "The Challenges of Combining Social and Commercial Enterprises," *Business Ethics Quarterly* (January 1998), 178.
2. Amelia Kohm and David LaPiana, *National Study of Strategic Restructuring among Nonprofit Organizations* (Chicago: Chapin Hall Center for Children at the University of Chicago, 2000). This study found that next to long-term planning needs, competition for funds was the main reason for NPO mergers.
3. Dees and Elias, 166.
4. See Karl Taro Greenfield, "A New Way of Giving," *Time* (July 24, 2000), 49–59, and Cheryl Dahle, "The Money and the Mission," *Fast Company* (April 2000), 172–184. For an academic treatment, see, for example, Sherri Leronda Wallace, "Social Entrepreneurship: The Role of Social Purpose Enterprises in Facilitating Community Economic Development," *Journal of Developmental Entrepreneurship,* vol. 4, no. 2 (Fall 1999), 153–174. Also, in 1999, the Kellogg Foundation produced a report on the emerging changes and challenges to philanthropy and social change organizations because of the introduction of market concepts to their work: "Unleashing New Resources and Entrepreneurship for the Common Good: A Scan, Synthesis, and Scenario for Action" (W.K. Kellogg Foundation, January 1999).
5. Carl Cannon, "Charity for Profit: How the New Social Entrepreneurs Are Creating Wealth by Creating Wealth," *National Journal,* no. 25 (June 17, 2000), 1899.
6. "Know thyself" was considered the primary maxim for, and first step toward, a moral life by ancient Greek and classical authors.
7. The U.S. median 1999 year-end hourly wage was $13.48 (Bureau of Labor Statistics, December 1999). State personal-income rankings taken from the 1999 edition of the *Statistical Abstract of the United States.*
8. See, for example, David Larson and Byron Johnson's *Religion: The Forgotten Factor in Cutting Youth Crime and Saving At-Risk Urban Youth,* intr. John DiIulio. Jeremiah Project paper 98-2 (New York: Manhattan Institute, 1998). The most extensive body of research on the relationship between religion and health is housed at the National Institute for Healthcare Research (www.nihr.org).
9. Interview with Vicky Church, February 2, 2000.
10. Gregory Dees again has offered a helpful overview of this situation in, "Enterprising Nonprofits," *Harvard Business Review* (January-February 1998), 54–66.

11 Over half of the trainees in the work-training program are previously unemployed parents of children within the Chicago Public School system, whose relationship with CCIL constitutes a substantial referral source. In 1999, for example, 91 of the 156 trainees in the program fit this category. Forty-one were residents at CCIL, and the remaining trainees were referred by other community organizations.

12 Christine Letts, William Ryan, and Allen Grossman, *Harvard Business Review* (March-April 1997), 36.49 Information for this section was supplied by John Brauer, executive director of CVE, in an interview, February 2, 2000.

13 Jed Emerson and Fay Twersky, *New Social Entrepreneurs: The Success, Challenge and Lessons of Nonprofit Enterprise Creation* (San Francisco: The Roberts Foundation, 1996), 1–2.

14 For a side-by-side comparison of conventional grant-making with REDF's approach, see the case study by Stanford University's Graduate School of Business, *The Roberts Enterprise Development Fund: Implementing a Social Venture Capital Approach to Philanthropy* (October 1998), Case S-E-45, p. 5.

15 *The Challenge of Change: Implementation of a Venture Philanthropy Strategy* (San Francisco: REDF & BTW Consultants), 8–10.

16 Information for this section was supplied by John Brauer, executive director of CVE, in an interview, February 2, 2000.

17 A full description of REDF's portfolio enterprises can be found at http://www.redf.org/about_portfolio.htm.

18 For an analysis of alternative credit markets in urban areas in particular, see Christie Baxter, "Canals Where Rivers Used to Flow: The Role of Mediating Structures and Partnerships in Community Lending," *Economic Development Quarterly* (February 1996), 44–56. The growing interest in and emphasis on individual development accounts (IDAs), which enable working poor families to save for home ownership, education, and business ventures, will also encourage locally driven efforts to encourage families to save money—or to put it another way, incentivize the accumulation of capital within individual households.

CHAPTER THREE
Building a Civic Infrastructure by Leveraging Local Intermediaries

The last chapter presented three different kinds of programs that exemplify new strategies for moving people toward economic and personal self-sufficiency. These kinds of programs are needed on a larger scale in response to the emerging tradition of devolution. In the present chapter, a couple of intermediaries are examined that have successfully leveraged organizational assets in a community. They also serve as promising models. They do not represent the only models that make a devolutionary society work well, but a community should pay close attention to them if it is to get the larger picture of service to low-income families right.

It is worth repeating that this book does not address the very important issues related to publicly funded programs for low-income communities, such as child care, transportation, food stamps, income-tax credits, housing vouchers, and so on. These are very important issues. This book is concerned, however, with encouraging communities to more aggressively build a civic infrastructure. The strength of a community's civic infrastructure—or those networks through which civic engagement is facilitated and human services delivered—will more or less determine how successfully these government programs are implemented. The kinds of relationships and services that are generated by the mechanisms described in this chapter build the social capital a community needs to deliver other services with the greatest degree of efficacy. A truly effective strategy for fighting poverty and the problems associated with it will give at least as much consideration to building valuable social capital in distressed communities as it will to providing direct economic relief.

The previous chapter described several programs aimed at bridging the gap between the mission and the market. They point us to the inestimable value in connecting networks of human services with occupational networks. The Jobs Partnership program, for instance, has just as much to do with connecting employer networks to urban church networks as it does connecting individuals to jobs. In the process of securing jobs for those who need them, the program is creating new relationships between formerly separated racial, economic, and social networks. The project of strengthening social capital in troubled areas requires that local markets and local communities be connected in ways that benefit both.

The Pillars of Civic Infrastructure

If the previous chapter had to do with innovations between the private for-profit and nonprofit sectors, the present chapter has to do with innovations between government and nonprofit-based communities of care. Given the significance—and recent popularity—of government collaborations with faith-based organizations (FBOs), this chapter will focus upon the important role of intermediary organizations in leveraging the strength of local religious organizations to help those outside the economic mainstream. Outreach by public officials and agencies to FBOs has become something of a movement sweeping across America, and like most early movements, it is occurring rather haphazardly. The purpose of this chapter is to look at a couple of examples that bring focus to the optimal way for the public sector to reach out to FBOs.

Enlarging and enriching the public square through the increased participation of FBOs in social service provision is only one important component of a healthy civic infrastructure. This chapter will focus exclusively on this component, but two additional components warrant mention and further study. They are (1) the use of community development corporations (CDCs) and (2) performance- and community-based social service contracting. Together with increased FBO involvement, they make up three essential pillars of a civic infrastructure. They are not the only pillars, but it is difficult to deny that without them a community is worse off. CDCs are perhaps the least known of the most significant community renewal efforts in America. They have begun to attract scholarly attention, and for this reason, this book will not add to the emerging body of work surrounding them. CDC activity in America can safely be called a large, established movement. Performance- and community-based social services contracting is far from a movement, but forward-looking urban reformers have experimented with it in cities such as Indianapolis, Milwaukee, and San Diego. And as outsourcing by government agencies to private companies continues to be a fast-growing trend (half of government spending is already going toward the purchase of goods and services in the private sector, and the numbers are growing[1]), the climate for performance contracting is as good as it has ever been. The merits of—and the difficulties encountered during—true performance-based social services contracting need to be rigorously studied and understood. The increased involvement of FBOs in social services is a movement somewhere between these two civic infrastructure pillars in both its magnitude and level of organization.

Any community that takes these three pillars seriously will have more well-kept houses, well-kept bodies, and well-kept souls. It is impossible to disconnect, for example, the success of Indianapolis as a community in the 1990s from the work of its fourteen very active CDCs, the reform of its private industry council into a manager of competition for job-related service provision, and its massive effort to place FBOs at the center of the city's assault on social problems (which will be described later). Indianapolis enjoys the second-lowest unemployment rate for metro areas in the United States, has watched some of its worst urban neighborhoods rebound back to life, and has seen its number of neighborhood associations boom across the city as citizens have become more engaged in their communities.

What is interesting about these three pillars is that none of them is entirely public or private in its operation and function. They all live and breathe within the world of transforming charity, in which multisector collaborations are ever more the norm. CDCs are private, and they receive a sub-

TRANSFORMING CHARITY

What They Are	What They Do	What They Contribute to the Civic Infrastructure
CDCs	CDCs are private, nonprofit organizations that build and provide affordable housing and invest in a range of improvement projects within a fixed urban or rural area. They are locally controlled, usually by residents of the neighborhood or area they serve. They receive funds from private and public sources.	*The Well-Kept House.* The bulk of CDCs' work is to provide affordable and rehabilitated housing. The outcome of their work is not only better conditions for residents but also increased business and real estate investment in and around the areas where they work. CDCs across the country have been responsible for stopping—and in some cases reversing—the slide of property values. They have given neighborhood residents the decision-making authority over development in their community that was once reserved for city planners and other private developers that understood their concerns too little.
Performance- and community-based contracting	This kind of contracting emphasizes two things: first, it demands results for services rendered, primarily for services responsible for helping people find and keep employment; second, it encourages or forces investment back into the community served by the contractors, either directly or indirectly by partnering with community-redeeming organizations.	*The Well-Kept Body.* The entire aim of social services is to help people get the food, shelter, and general care they need—either by providing these things directly or, better, preparing people to provide them for themselves. Performance contracting with a strong community focus forces government to pay attention to these outcomes rather than the processes of the programs themselves. A preoccupation with program processes is the perennial sin of government social services that performance contracting is designed to eliminate. It forces public agencies to remember why they exist.
FBO Social Networks	Faith-based organization social networks include houses of worship as well as independent religious organizations providing community-redeeming services of varying sorts in partnership with each other and a variety of other private and even public organizations.	*The Well-Kept Soul.* FBOs have always made the upkeep of the soul their main concern. They are now in increasing numbers expressing this concern through social services that are publicly respected by people outside their particular confession and sometimes viewed as nontraditional within their confession. Their greater involvement in public matters also brings with it an enriched public discussion of values and moral habits.

Figure A: Three Pillars of a Solid Civic Infrastructure

stantial amount of funding from a varied list of private supporters. One impressive private intermediary organization, the Local Initiative Support Corporation (which has recently enjoyed increased attention since former Treasury Secretary Robert Rubin became its chairman) is a $300 million operation whose exclusive purpose is to provide resources to CDCs in thirty-eight cities and sixty-six rural communities.[2] But CDCs also receive substantial public funding as well as investment through tax credit incentives, and they work with their local public community development agencies. In cities where they are most active, they have become a mainstay of the local government's community development policies and have changed the politics of development considerably. There are currently four thousand CDCs nationwide providing upward of 50,000 affordable houses and apartments every year. Below-market interest rates are made possible by blended public-private financing, which then usually attracts larger private investment.[3]

Performance-contracting can only be initiated by public agencies, but when it is successful, it is partially due to partnerships that the provider establishes with community-based organizations. In order to perform up to the terms of the contract, the service providers need to get as much help for the people they are serving as possible. Part of the reason, however, performance contracting has had trouble becoming a movement is because it ultimately places greater pressure on public agencies. Few public administrations are willing to raise standards on themselves. The few that have successfully done so implemented performance contracting in light of welfare reform, as they felt the pressure to reduce their welfare rolls. But now that people have moved off welfare faster than anyone expected, the best performance cultures may be in jeopardy today as their opponents argue that they are no longer necessary. If these opponents succeed, in the end, it will be the people receiving services who will suffer—which is what almost always happens when government agencies relax their performance standards. The success of social service delivery is not, as some have advocated, merely a function of devolving responsibility to private sector charities. Government has long given over service delivery to the private sector at federal, state, and local levels.[4] Successful delivery occurs when results are placed at a premium and a performance culture is designed toward that end. In Milwaukee, for example, service providers are required to invest a portion of their profits back into community-redeeming initiatives and organizations. By its nature, performance contracting, in which community involvement is part of the performance criteria, drives the construction of a civic infrastructure.

As the two case studies in this chapter indicate, FBOs can play an impressive role in the public effort to reduce poverty, fight crime, and improve their communities. What is needed is the creative use of intermediaries to rally FBOs together around a particular issue or as a general force for good or both. The more we see such intermediaries, the more we can expect to see an increasingly coherent movement in America to expand the role of FBOs. Much like the CDC movement, which has expanded community development beyond government halls into neighborhoods and has attracted investment from capital markets once nervous about getting too close to blighted areas, the emerging movement of socially engaged FBOs is expanding our notion of the public square. Intermediary organizations have a significant role to play in making the public square a safe and welcoming place for FBOs. They leverage FBOs' greatest strengths without endangering the special separation of public and religious institutions that is the hallmark of religious liberty and political reasonableness in the United States.

This last issue is important enough to draw attention to it briefly. There are a number of legitimate reasons to be concerned that this movement will generate violations of the First Amendment. These concerns should continually be addressed, and the movement should continually be assessed in light of them. There are also a lot of illegitimate arguments against the movement, which are rooted more in ideology than experience. For instance, fears that FBOs will become enslaved to government bureaucracies underestimate the great care and caution that most FBOs demonstrate whenever they attempt to work in partnership with government. And as will be indicated later, partnerships between public agencies and religious groups take on many forms, many of which involve no financial transactions. Also, available preliminary research shows that these partnerships are working responsibly within the bounds of the First Amendment and that in most local areas, the church-state issue is largely a nonissue to all the parties involved.[5] These partnerships are resulting in people leaving poverty—not in their being subjected to religious coercion. Local communities witness the results and appreciate the partnerships that produce the results. It is usually ideology more than experience with such partnerships that leads detractors to argue against them.

Why is building civic infrastructure important in a world of transforming charity? Research on adults in poverty—together with a number of failed federal programming experiments—suggests that the road out of poverty has as much to do with peoples' aspirations, esteem, and access to opportunity as their technical skills. Analysis of the National Longitudinal Survey of Youth (NLSY), for instance, suggests that young adults in poverty struggle more to generate higher earnings over time the lower their academic and professional aspirations, their sense of self-worth, and their access to core sectors in the marketplace.[6] Communities of support and new portals to the workforce are of utmost importance in today's world. Federal spending in the United States on programs for the working poor has increased tremendously in the past two decades. If communities are not rebuilding their infrastructure, such spending may not achieve its intended results.

As Figure B shows, the increase in spending for working poor Americans is largely due to the Earned Income Tax Credit, which is a refundable sliding-scale credit that can boost working poor household incomes significantly, and to the growth of health care spending.[7] These programs provide substantial relief from the effects of poverty, and in so far as they encourage work, they are doubly useful. They do little, however, *to change the position of the working poor in the world* in terms of giving them avenues to exercise their aspirations and thereby move out of poverty. And without a strong civic infrastructure, working poor families lack the social networks and opportunity to get the skills, resources, and assistance that can move them into economic stability. They are, essentially, left to themselves, perhaps with a little more money in their pockets, but without the networks that can help them succeed in the long run.

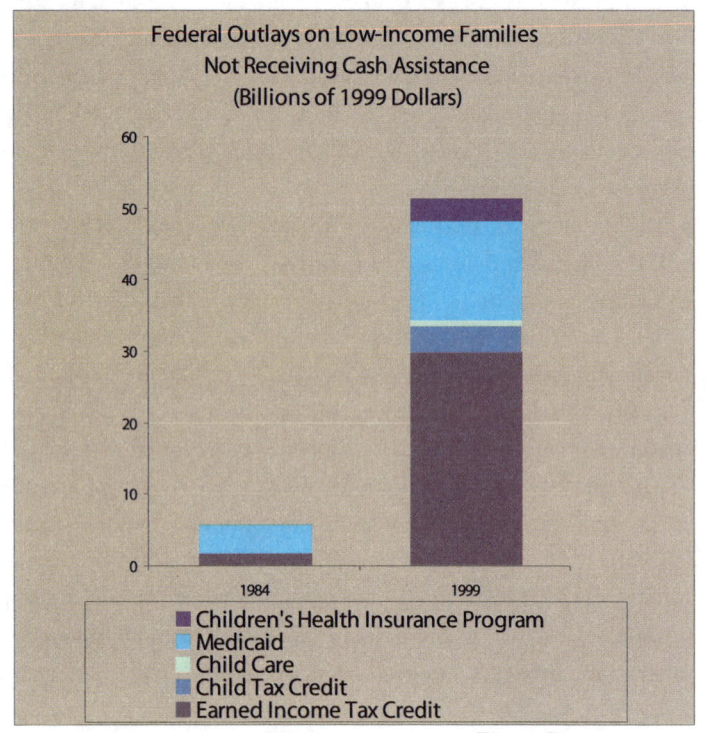

Federal Outlays on Low-Income Families Not Receiving Cash Assistance (Billions of 1999 Dollars)

- Children's Health Insurance Program
- Medicaid
- Child Care
- Child Tax Credit
- Earned Income Tax Credit

Figure B

Without such a civic infrastructure, the poor are subject to an overly *economic*—and not moral and social—idea of poverty relief. An overly economic view of poverty assumes that more money and supportive resources equals poverty relief. In a world of transformed charity, if the poor are to be helped to advance out of poverty, multisector collaborations such as those described in the previous and present chapters of this book will open or close the door to their future.

Whose Job Is It to Help Those Left Behind?

The answer to this question is complex. The most general and uncontroversial—and perhaps unhelpful—answer is, "those who are most able." But recent history has seen an emerging consensus define "those who are most able" as "those who are closest to those in need and who have a stake in helping them." Each of the three previously described "pillars" is built upon the idea that community-based design and delivery of important services helps communities fare better. This chapter focuses upon the role of FBOs in this mix. Good written work has already begun to emerge on the growth of CDCs. Contrarily, hardly any good work has been done on effective performance contracting. This needs to be done. With regard to FBO social networks, much good is being done "on the ground" by individual organizations and partnerships, but not enough work has been produced on the role of *intermediaries* in building those networks. Given how important well-kept souls are to a community, what follows is a contribution to this growing and ongoing discussion.

One of the most significant achievements during the 1990s was the height to which public debate took religious organizations as a forgotten answer to the question, "whose job is it to help those left behind?" While they are not the *sole* caregiver, FBOs are in the business of caring for the deepest and most personal needs people have. As a consensus began to form in the early 1990s that nothing short of personal transformation could help some of our gravest social pathologies, FBOs entered the public square as the "last great hope." The welfare reform act of 1996 contains an increasingly well-known Charitable Choice clause allowing federal funds to go to FBOs while allowing the organizations to maintain a considerable amount of religious autonomy. This law, rather than the start of a change in public opinion, was really the capstone of a two-decade effort to increase the role of FBOs in social service provision. Already in 1982, President Ronald Reagan had called for greater social service provision among FBOs and less from government agencies. By 1996, Democrats as well as Republicans had embraced the idea that care could best administered by those who were close to those in need, especially if the caregivers had a religious commitment.

The sources of this emerging consensus were numerous. Members of Congress visited faith-based programs in their home districts and saw amazing results that they conveyed to their colleagues. Some religious organizations began calling themselves and their brethren to a broader social demonstration of their faith. Various academics and public intellectuals began writing about the social significance of FBOs and criticizing the prevailing elite prejudice against them. The consensus did not emerge based on the conclusions of hard scientific research as it did, for instance, in the case of the medical community's growing acceptance of faith as a legitimate variable in wellness.[8] So far, the best model studies on the social significance of faith are those organized by the University of Pennsylvania's John DiIulio: *Religion: The Forgotten Factor in Cutting Youth Crime and Saving At-Risk Urban Youth*, and *A Better Kind of High: How Religious Commitment Reduces Drug Use Among Poor Urban Teens*.[9] More studies of this sort are needed so that we understand what kinds of FBOs succeed, how they succeed, and how they best partner with related public efforts.

The movement to involve FBOs in solving social welfare problems has thus come from what most Americans are confident in claiming about them: FBOs are usually in close physical proximity to those in need, and they offer as part of their *essence* a moral commitment and compassion that secular programs do not (or if the latter do, they do so not essentially but accidentally, as a function of the character of a caseworker here and a compassionate administrator there but not as a fundamental part of the program design or philosophy). When federal welfare programs began in the 1930s, they were built upon the expectation that one's family would take primary responsibility for providing a "safety net" of support and aid. The federal programs were a supplement to what was lacking in the family. In today's fractured subcultures of poverty, particularly in their densest manifestation in cities, the predominantly single-parent families often provide whatever support they can, but they are already under tremendous financial and emotional stresses. These families themselves need help, or even transformation.

The recent movement to include FBOs in the public process is something of an attempt to have them fill in the gaps in broken families. Thus FBOs are currently being called upon to take up a daunting two-pronged mission: to rebuild families and to provide needed resources. It is, of course, unrealistic to expect them to accomplish both very well or very quickly. And yet, in the areas of the United States where poverty is most intractable and its effects most malicious, FBOs often represent the *only* community assets capable of helping people out of poverty. They are often the only community-based organizations that have both the hand of compassion to encourage people to higher ground and the moral authority to make demands of them on the journey. And so long as we subscribe to a view of poverty that is more than economic but includes the role of habits in prolonging poverty, we must take this unique capability of FBOs seriously.

None of this should suggest, as it is often interpreted to suggest, that FBOs are in demand because general public consensus has asked too much of them. They have increasingly been taking social service provision on themselves over the past two decades, well in advance of the Charitable Choice clause that made public funding for those services more easily available to them. The first significant national study on the expanded scope of FBO–provided social services was conducted by Independent Sector in 1988. The study showed that religious organizations were contributing significantly to the social welfare of their communities. But they were doing more. The authors remarked that "congregations not only engage in religious ministry and education but are deeply involved in serving their members and communities across a broad area of activities. The natural affinity between religious belief and improving the human condition is *probably much stronger than people think*. Almost as many congregations offer programs in human services, 87 percent, as offer religious services and religious education."[10] A 1993 follow-up study of the same name by Independent Sector confirmed the same, if only to show more convincingly that FBOs were providing a substantial amount of social services.

The trend is continuing.[11] The most recent study to examine the impact of the Charitable Choice clause on FBOs found that it has significantly encouraged the initiation of new partnerships between government agencies and FBOs. The study, conducted by Hudson Institute's Amy Sherman and published by The Center for Public Justice, found that 57 percent of the partnerships involved FBOs that had never formerly cooperated with government. Only 51 percent of all the partnerships included in the study were direct financial collaborations in which the FBO held a contract with a local public agency. Sixteen percent were indirect financial arrangements in which the FBOs served as subcontractors to an intermediary that held a contract with a public agency, and the remaining 33 percent were non-financial collaborations in which cooperation was formal but did not include any payments to the FBOs.[12] These findings suggest not only that new partnerships are on the rise, but that they are far more complex than most theorists usually think. The number of non-financial collaborations is evidence of a willingness on the part of FBOs to join hands with the public square for reasons having more to do with their stated mission to serve the needy than their financial concerns alone.

It is too soon to know in exact terms how well these new collaborations are faring and what kinds of results they are producing. As the extensive research conducted by Ram Cnaan has revealed, though religious social service providers are widely active in America, academic literature and research on them is terribly (and unfairly) scarce, let alone research on partnerships between public agencies and FBOs that provide social services.[13] What is even scarcer is the use of evaluative agendas that attempt to account for the relationship of the spiritual—and thus heightened moral—aspect of FBO programs and the results produced by them.[14] But what is clear is that we have witnessed a rise in the role of FBOs as contributors to our overall social welfare. They are strategically (both in terms of geography and in terms of the moral community they provide) situated to help those in need and are, in general, accepting their situation willingly.

Without a doubt momentum is carrying forward the publicly favorable perception of FBOs. It is not without significance that the 2000 presidential race made the issue of government partnerships with FBOs one of its first. Al Gore voiced his support for such partnerships in May 1999, and then George W. Bush launched his campaign two months later with a speech that laid out plans to place FBOs squarely in the game of social service provision. President Clinton even got on board with the idea in September 1999, and spoke of an "emerging consensus" about the issue and said that FBO participation provides an enhanced "leverage of the good things that the government is funding."[15] And President Bush established the White House Office for Faith-based and Community Initiatives almost immediately upon assuming office in 2001. The number of faith-based initiatives that have popped up in major federal agencies and in state agencies across the nation is further evidence that the new acceptance of religion's voice in the public square is more than a passing fad.

We may be, as E. J. Dionne suggests, in the midst of another great renegotiation of faith's relationship to public life in which we are jointly confessing that the past half century has been too hostile to religion and has unnecessarily kept it from influencing the general public in ways that are constitutionally legitimate.[16] The recent trend in the courts toward a neutrality interpretation of the First Amendment—that is, that the government should treat all groups equally with regard to eligibility for receiving funds, so long as those groups serve the secular purpose for which those funds are available—has served to strengthen Dionne's thesis and to give a green light to the numerous faith-based government initiatives cited earlier.[17]

FBOs are not the complete answer to the question, "Whose job is it to help those left behind?" But the effort to make their place in society more noble and of greater public significance is important and helps make a larger point. The full answer to the question is the *community as a whole*, not primarily government or other traditional nonprofit helping organizations alone. One of the travesties of the welfare state that emerged in the 1960s is the virtual quarantine of the poor from the rest of the community in special housing and by special programs requiring them not to be a part of the local mainstream economy if they wished to maintain their public benefits. The recent situation of FBOs represents a larger opportunity to build entire communities of support that look and feel much different than the iron safety net of the welfare state that made it difficult for people to escape. A new civic infrastructure is needed that situates responsibility for the poor on each member of a community according to that member's role and specific capacity.

The following section will look at intermediaries that can help leverage the work of smaller community-based organizations in general, and FBOs in particular. But if we are to build a new civic structure, government must be forced to redefine its unique role according to where its strengths lie. With regard to services for the poor, government agencies are best positioned primarily as brokers of services and secondarily as providers of them. Government should perform this function at least as much out of its unique role as custodian of the public square as out of its need to be efficient and keep costs down.

Between the Heavenly City and the Earthly City: Intermediary Organizers

Throughout Western history, the "heavenly city" has been the symbol toward which religious activity is aimed. The "earthly city" has been the domain of political and economic affairs. The heavenly city is "not of this world," and its institutions often do not run according to the expectations of the earthly city. The nature of contractual agreements, deadlines, measurable outcomes, and rigorous accounting are frequently lost upon religious organizations. In so far as they design their activity to partner with and positively impact the earthly city, however, they need to create within themselves the mechanisms with which the earthly city is familiar.

One of the most widely discussed issues concerning the rise of FBOs' public involvement concerns their lack of capacity. What do people mean by "capacity"? Essentially, capacity refers to the organizational ability of the FBOs to access the opportunities available to them, manage relations with public and other agencies, and properly fill out reporting requirements and other formal documentation. Religious groups are usually by their very nature flexible in their operation, and those that are providing an above-average number of socially redeeming services are often the same ones in low-income urban neighborhoods that have limited staff and resources.[18] Their mission is to serve people. They reserve bookkeeping for whatever free time they can grab, and they usually have little to no experience in applying for grants. Of course, one major issue behind concerns about organizational capacity is the potential that, through missteps due to ignorance or even carelessness, FBOs will violate the church-state relationship. But the more common reason for concern about FBO capacity is simply that, despite their effectiveness in serving people, they may eventually fail to perform well as a service provider and thus be removed from consideration as a community partner. Universal performance standards must be upheld, and grassroots organizations will remain unappealing partners to the extent that they are unorganized or unaccountable or both.

This concern has led to an acknowledgment that relationships with FBOs and other community-based organizations need to be facilitated in a special way. On the one hand, they need to be positioned to do what they do best, while on the other hand, they need help in the capacity areas where they are weak. Here are three of the most widely discussed structures for facilitating government partnership with FBOs:

1. *National Umbrella:* UCLA's James Q. Wilson has speculated that a parallel "United Way–like" organization for FBOs could be instituted.[19] The purpose of this organization would be to provide a way for federal funding to go to a neutral national organization that would then identify effective faith-based efforts to support through a network of local chapters.

2. *Community-Based Intermediary Organization:* In communities across America, a number of local organizations exist to mobilize area congregations to provide an array of services. The intermediaries, which are usually charitable organizations that have credibility within the religious community, hold a contract with the government to serve a predetermined number of welfare clients. They are responsible to administer the contract, but congregations and other FBOs that they recruit deliver the services to the clients.

3. *Government Facilitator:* The new White House Office of Faith-Based and Community Initiatives is an experiment in setting up a federally sponsored quasi-intermediary between federal agencies and community organizations. Indianapolis' Front Porch Alliance is an example of a local government acting as a community coordinator for FBOs. Under Mayor Stephen Goldsmith's leadership, the Front Porch Alliance, a government-funded entity

within the mayoral administration, assisted FBOs in leveraging funding, forming effective partnerships, and accessing critical government services, and helped bring the voice of FBOs to the policy-making table. Another commonly used strategy is to appoint faith liaisons within an administration or agency whose sole job it is to build alliances with FBOs within a community or across a state. Many states and localities are already doing this. Texas has appointed faith liaisons in each of its ten human services districts and is to date the most sophisticated example of this strategy.

The first proposal is theoretical and does not currently exist in practice. It holds great potential but also great challenges. It might create a large bureaucratic organization less responsive to local needs than might be hoped, but it could also bring a great amount of weight and centrality to the importance of socially redeeming FBO initiatives.

The locally based intermediary and government facilitator models do in fact exist and have been implemented with some success at the local level. On the national scene, the new White House Office of Faith-Based and Community Initiatives marks the first attempt to set up a government facilitator model for the United States as a whole. While some fear it will only increase the likelihood of constitutional problems, it provides help to FBOs by promoting them as welcome additions to the general public effort to improve the social welfare of millions of Americans and by eliminating structural barriers to their participation in public contracting processes.[20] The intermediaries that have been around for a while are products of local communities and administrations. If the developing public enthusiasm for involving FBOs more directly in the public process is to continue, we need to understand the nature of these partnerships. This chapter will look at examples of each; both examples have received national attention for their innovative character and success. Each represents the best way to focus and leverage the power contained in a community's FBOs while maintaining constitutional checks that protect both church and state from illegal entanglement with each other.

CHAPTER THREE

Intermediary Type	Advantages	Disadvantages
National Umbrella	‡ Its scale makes disparate levels of quality in localities less likely ‡ Independence as an organization would create consistency over time ‡ Strong organizational capacity	‡ Likely to be expensive, tying up funds in operations
Locally Based Intermediary Organization	‡ Provides a clear "buffer" between government and FBOs ‡ Usually provides better administrative capacity than individual FBOs at less cost than government administration	‡ Is often detached from local government agencies, other contractors providing similar services, etc.
Government Facilitator	‡ Puts government in best position for ensuring constitutional adherence and government-side support for FBOs ‡ Provides the best link between local "street-level" knowledge about programs that work and government	‡ Is dependent on the current administration ‡ May easily become a bureaucratic agent within government

Figure C: Advantages and Disadvantages of Three Intermediary Structures

The Effective Community Intermediary: Ottawa County Good Samaritan

University of Arizona professor Mark Chaves' National Congregations Study has shown that although large congregations spend more money on social services (one percent of churches in the study, or those with more than 900 members, spend 25 percent of all money spent by churches on social services), the average congregation providing social services has seventy-five people and has a budget of $55,000.[21] As pointed out earlier, congregations in poor urban areas do more than the average congregation, and many of them fit this size and budget description all too well. What this means, of course, is that they are hardly equipped to manage a relationship—not to mention a contract—with a public agency without some help.

Though there is currently much written about building capacity in FBOs and other nonprofit organizations as a solution to this problem, it is unlikely that their capacity will be increased to the degree that is needed for them to assume the bulk of administrative responsibility for social services currently overseen by public agencies. It is not implausible, however, to imagine FBOs supplying a greater share of actual service provision. In any event, it is also legitimate to ask whether or not they should take on greater responsibility for social service delivery solely because public agencies are presenting them an "opportunity" to work in partnership. What they do best, they do because of a commitment to a mission grounded in faith, and any choice to enhance their organizational capacity should extend from this commitment alone.

An intermediary organization in the community, which knows the "lay of the land" and already has an adequate management infrastructure, makes the best partner for public agencies. It was mentioned earlier that a number of states are appointing liaisons to the faith community in public agencies. This has value in itself as a way to provide outreach from a government office to FBOs and to coordinate action where their common interests overlap. But an effective intermediary that has already built networks within the faith community will likely do the best job of coordinating FBOs around a common project. Liaisons, actually, would be greatly aided by the identification of effective intermediaries.

CHAPTER THREE

Good Samaritan Ministries of Ottawa County, Michigan, functions as an intermediary between the county welfare agency and area churches. Founded by area churches in 1969 to serve the needs of Mexican immigrants, it initially operated on a "center-based" model of ministry in which people physically came to the organization for help. In the 1970s churches began sending people with needs to Good Samaritan, which made the organization's leaders reconsider their way of doing things. Why should churches, who historically have had the responsibility of helping people, send them down the road to another organization? Good Samaritan began gathering churches together around ministry opportunities that it administered, but in which the churches themselves delivered help to those in need. Already in the late 1980s, Good Samaritan had designed "family support programs" in which church members were trained as mentors to help the needy who came through its doors. By the time of welfare reform in the 1990s, it was well positioned to assist the county move its welfare recipients to work by providing a well-coordinated mentoring support system.

Ottawa County gained national attention when it became the first county in America to reduce its welfare caseload to zero. It was the best performing of Michigan's six pilot sites in the state's Project Zero, a comprehensive program to move families from welfare to work and eventually to freedom from government assistance. The county has 210,000 residents and began Project Zero with 175 families on welfare. One year after Project Zero was launched, over 90 percent of Ottawa County's welfare recipients had earnings from work, by far the highest of the pilot sites, and the overall caseload had declined 60 percent in the county, far in front of the second-place site, which had a 45 percent decline. But most significant was the fact that of those welfare recipients who had secured employment, *none* had returned to welfare. This remarkable feat was unrivaled by the second-best performing site, which saw 32 percent return to welfare within the first year (see Figure D).[22]

In the State of Michigan's official one-year evaluation, Ottawa County was acknowledged for having effectively eliminated child care as a barrier to employment and for having the best transportation assistance for welfare

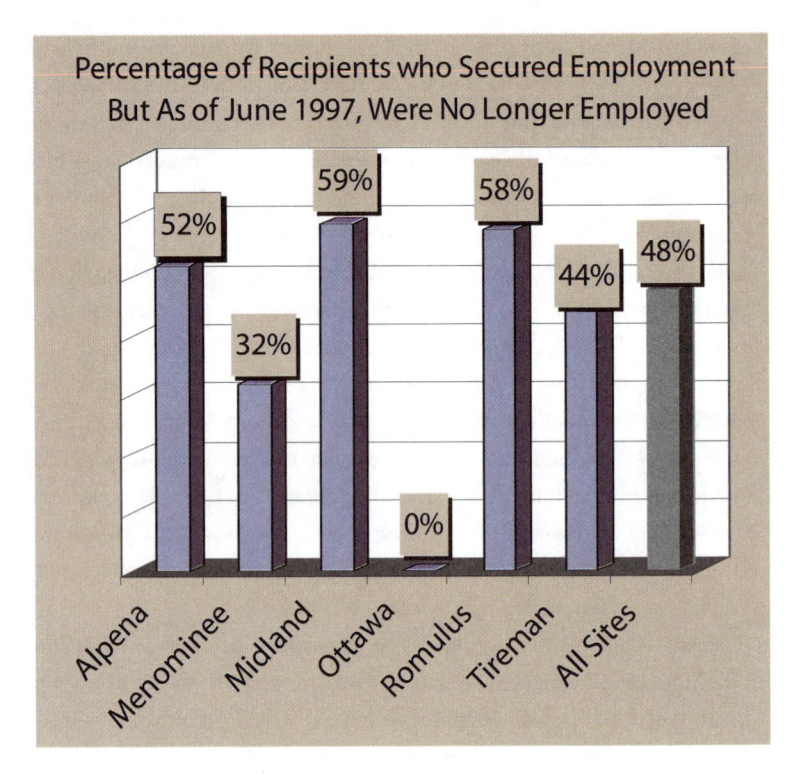

Percentage of Recipients who Secured Employment But As of June 1997, Were No Longer Employed

- Alpena: 52%
- Menominee: 32%
- Midland: 59%
- Ottawa: 0%
- Romulus: 58%
- Tireman: 44%
- All Sites: 48%

Figure D
Source: State of Michigan Family Independence Agency, 1997

recipients—the two problems most cited by the county's welfare recipients as significant barriers to self-sufficiency early in Project Zero's implementation.[23]

What is the reason given by the State of Michigan for Ottawa's success? *Mentoring services.* Project Zero's official evaluation remarks, "Ottawa [County] cited mentoring services as a key resource in assisting clients toward self-sufficiency. It provided a host of services to assist recipients in gaining and maintaining employment. The mentors met the crucial need of reducing individual family barriers and provided a support network for families."[24] The evaluation continues to stress that while mentoring shows great possibility as a means of helping move families to self-sufficiency, it is highly dependent upon the local community's strategy and ability to mobilize local volunteers and resources.

Good Samaritan led the way in Ottawa County's mentoring strategy. At the start of Project Zero the county contracted Good Samaritan's services for one year for $102,000. Its contract has been renewed three times since then, each time at lower amounts proportionate to the number of people requiring service in the county. Its role as an intermediary was to recruit churches from the county as partners in the effort to help welfare recipients move to self-sufficiency. Since Project Zero began, Good Samaritan has received 265 client referrals from the Ottawa County social services agency and has had sixty-one churches involved in mentoring relationships. Half of the referrals became involved in sustained mentoring relationships. Church mentors and welfare recipients were asked to commit to a six-to twelve-month relationship. The average length of the mentoring relationships has been seven months. Relationships continued in some cases up to fourteen months.

The churches mobilized 665 volunteers to serve as mentors. Good Samaritan estimates that the volunteers have given 20,496 hours of their time during the four years it has worked with the county welfare agency. According to Independent Sector's estimated hourly value of volunteer services, Ottawa County received more than $287,559 of assistance from the church mentors.[25] This, of course, does not even consider donated goods and other services provided by the churches and mentors to the families they were serving. Good Samaritan estimates this amount to be greater than $58,000.

When it first received its contract with the county, Good Samaritan began working with its preestablished network of churches. Its staff visited churches and outlined a vision for helping reduce welfare dependency in the county. "We said to churches, 'If you don't think the current welfare system works, would you be willing to be a part of the solution?'" remembers Executive Director Janet De Young. Good Samaritan designed a training model based on the feedback from the churches. And for those churches that responded "yes" to the question De Young and her colleagues posed, Good Samaritan held training sessions to prepare mentors to understand the problems poor families face, design problem-solving strategies, come alongside a family without doing all the work for them, and help with financial planning and debt reduction.

Mentors and welfare recipients were then brought together to sign an agreement that outlined goals and established responsibilities for each of the parties. De Young says that at least as much time has been spent working with volunteers and churches as on any other aspect of the contract. "Mentors often do not know how to respond appropriately to families moving from welfare to work and therefore need a lot of training and help themselves," she remarks. Good Samaritan devotes one to two highly qualified full-time staff members to the effort.

None of the money received by the nonprofit from the county passes down to the churches. This arrangement was perfectly acceptable to the churches, who were generally uninterested in wedding themselves contractually to the state. Good Samaritan's contracts have been on a reimbursement basis according to approved activities such as recruiting mentors, assessing family need, and providing specialized help to families when appropriate. All these activities fall under a First Amendment condition that states that Good Samaritan "may not under any circumstances deny services to eligible clients on the basis of faith" and "shall not actively proselytize" in any of the activities covered under the scope of the contract.

So successful has Good Samaritan been at recruiting and training mentors from churches that new opportunities to creatively tackle post-welfare issues have arisen. Now that the majority of the welfare population is working, other issues such as the lack of transportation and adequate housing are the most pronounced barriers to independence, as they are in communities across the country. Ottawa County was dissatisfied with current approaches to helping low-income families find adequate transportation and approached Good Samaritan in 1999 to see if the intermediary could craft a community-based solution to the problem. With a start-up grant from the county and with its well-established network among churches and the community at large, Good Samaritan launched CarLink, Inc., a nonprofit subsidiary, complete with a used-car dealer's license, to provide donated automobiles for families lacking transportation. Roughly one out of every five cars it receives from donors is in good enough shape to be made roadworthy for two years without much expense. The remaining 80 percent of the cars are sold, and the earnings are used to pay for maintenance on the cars that go to the families in need. CarLink, Inc., is on the road to becoming a fully self-supporting operation. In just one year, 120 cars were donated, and by the end of 2000, forty families have received an automobile that they otherwise would have had to live without. Of these forty, thirty of them are welfare-to-work families referred to Good Samaritan through Project Zero.

CarLink, Inc., is a great example of a community partnership. Putting its solid mentoring history to continued use, Good Samaritan has arranged for mentors from the community's churches to help prepare the recipient family for the responsibilities of car ownership. The relationship begins before the expectant car owner actually acquires the car, so that he or she can be fully equipped to understand everything from auto insurance to regular maintenance schedules. Local radio stations run free ads for the program, and marketers have given of their time to make sure the entire community becomes aware of CarLink's purpose and operation. A local ministry provides auto detailing and quarterly oil changes for the new car owners, and area auto dealers provide repair service at reduced rates and often supply parts at cost so that the transition into car ownership can be as seamless as possible. One of the dealers provides the space for the donated cars before they are repaired or sold. Mike Hamilton, Good Samaritan's director of ministries, says, "There is no way we could feasibly run CarLink without the community partnerships we've got in place." Ottawa County is showing, once again, that a broadly scaled, well-coordinated community solution can be drafted for a serious problem facing the poor that provides good service at negligible costs to the community. The program has also created a sense of purpose and pride in a community that has shown a remarkable commitment to taking responsibility for poverty as an entire community.

TRANSFORMING CHARITY

But this is not all. In 1995, Good Samaritan and two other community organizations began working with churches to address the need for transitional housing in their community for their homeless clients. They recognized that the move from homelessness to home ownership required an intermediary step, transitional housing, of which their community had little. So they asked the churches to consider making properties they owned, often adjacent to their church property, available as transitional housing. The Community Housing Partnership was born, in which homeless individuals and families were provided with housing for two years. During these two years, they have a mentor supplied by the church to help them prepare for home ownership. Good Samaritan leases the properties from the churches below market rate. Until recently, the program worked with thirteen properties. But because of its success, and because of the overall reputation that Good Samaritan has built for itself, it has received a three-year, $1 million grant from the U.S. Department for Housing and Urban Development (HUD) to scale the program up to thirty-one properties. The grant also allows Good Samaritan to lease the properties from churches at market rate and rent them out to the occupants at 30 percent of their current income. Most of the properties are church-owned. The program's success, combined with its positive image in the community, has led some churches to purchase properties exclusively for the program.

In the year 2000, three out of six new Habitat for Humanity home owners in Ottawa County were graduates of the Community Housing Partnership. In October 2000, Good Samaritan saw its ninth family move from homelessness to home ownership. Other families have moved into rental situations but are in equally good financial shape. With the HUD–sponsored expansion, these impressive numbers can be expected to rise even more.

Good Samaritan is a robust example of how a community-based intermediary can help a community navigate the waters of our post-welfare reform world. Unlike many older war-on-poverty-style programs, which placed funding and processes above relationships, it has built its success upon relationships rather than treating them as an add-on to what is perceived as an already sufficient service. It has not done this without adequate funding and effective processes, but relationship-building has been its centerpiece. It has built relationships with the community, and it has enabled mentors to build relationships with families that need the kind of help no process or funding can provide of itself.

It may be objected that Good Samaritan is a fine model for a place like Ottawa County, Michigan, but that it will not work in other, more complex settings. Ottawa County is, compared to urban counties with entrenched poverty and higher per capita welfare caseloads, a fairly homogeneous region with a fairly strong economic history. This should not discredit Good Samaritan's work. The fact that the county was the first in the nation to bring its caseload to zero is enough to quiet any such objections. Good Samaritan represents an intermediary model that sets its poverty-fighting focal point on relationships rather than programs, responsibility rather than dependence. It is a model of transformed charity in which the local welfare delivery structure was radically changed. The expectations placed upon welfare recipients challenged the community as a whole to succeed in making economic independence available to *everyone*. Communities and agencies that do not understand the relational basis of this kind of transformed charity will, most likely, fail to happily surf upon the increasingly complex "wake of welfare reform" discussed in the first chapter. They will remain stuck in an older type of charity, justified by their good intentions but at the expense of the poor.

Government Facilitator: The Front Porch Alliance

The strength of Good Samaritan as an intermediary lies in its ability to rally churches around important poverty issues facing its community. It leverages the contribution churches have to make without requiring them to administer a state contract or programs requiring processes alien to the churches' unique cultures. And in its role as a well-respected, faith-based intermediary, it serves as a buffer between government and individual congregations. Were the local government to directly enlist the services of several of the churches apart from Good Samaritan's help, the likelihood of church-state conflicts, real or perceived, would likely increase.

Another proven mechanism for an effective interface between government and the faith community is a government-sponsored, quasi-intermediary such as Indianapolis' Front Porch Alliance (FPA). Former Indianapolis mayor Stephen Goldsmith launched FPA in 1997 as an endeavor to empower faith-based and other community organizations to take the lead in solving the city's most intractable social problems. FPA continued its activity through the end of 1999, when Goldsmith left office and his successor discontinued its activity in 2000. FPA provided FBOs with help in accessing public and private resources, cutting through city bureaucracy when it interfered with their work, and building the capacity in their organizations so that they were better equipped in the future to serve their communities. The initiative created a flurry of activity and produced early victories, which captured the attention of a diverse set of policy makers and journalists across the nation.

It also created a stir at home. Within one year, FPA had a 25 percent name recognition in Indianapolis, more than almost any other city hall initiative. The reason? Community leaders, pastors, and public officials agree that FPA was clearly an effort to put residents and neighborhoods first in all social policy deliberations. In the words of one neighborhood leader, "Working from the principle that government must first do no harm to the institutions of civil society, [FPA] enables [faith-based and community organizations] to expand the good work they already do."[26] Bill Stanczykiewicz, Goldsmith's former community policy director and originator of FPA's design, says, "We knew when we started that lots of inner-city congregations were legitimately skeptical of city hall. Our first job, which was typical of Goldsmith's style, was to go sit with them and ask them what we needed to do to make them succeed—since they are the ones that can truly bring healing to our city in ways government cannot." According to Goldsmith, trust was built up in three ways. First, his office set up a citizen-driven advisory board and consulted numerous organizations before FPA was officially launched. Second, his administration put its full support behind FBOs early in the process and produced results instead of mere rhetoric. And third, he built up the FPA staff to make it hyper-responsive to requests from FBOs and other community organizations.[27] FPA's rapid success is remarkable considering that it was based in the mutual respect and cooperation between Goldsmith, a Jewish Republican, and mainly African American pastors, almost all of whom are lifelong Democrats.

FPA established partnerships with more than five hundred churches and other organizations in the Indianapolis area. In less than two years it directly distributed over $350,000 to organizations in the community running socially redeeming programs, and it has assisted organizations to write proposals that resulted in nearly $500,000 in funding. For every dollar FPA invested into its outreach efforts, three additional dollars were leveraged from public and private sources. Dedicated to empowering communities to fight crime and help youth, FPA was a critical player in launching the Indianapolis Ten Point Coalition, a group of more than thirty churches that provide street patrols in high-crime areas, educational programs for youth, and employment opportunities for at-risk young people. It is perhaps the most sophisticated and successful of the various Ten Point Coalitions across the nation, second only to the original program in Boston, founded by the charismatic urban pastor, Reverend Eugene Rivers.

FPA provided assistance to Indianapolis' largest teen abstinence program, which—considered apart from other FPA-supported youth activities—has involved more than four thousand youth in both private and public schools. It has assisted numerous organizations to finance and provide programming, the majority of which is in the summer when youth are most vulnerable to the vagaries of inner-city "free time," for nearly five thousand Indianapolis youth. FPA has facilitated partnerships between more than thirty churches and twenty public schools. The partnerships provide tutoring, after-school programming, and mentoring for the students.

FPA helped a pastor close down a crack house and start a drug relapse prevention center in its place by leveraging available funds and navigating through the requisite red tape. It has helped found a near eastside business association, which is chaired by a local pastor, comprised of over sixty members, and dedicated to revitalizing the surrounding neighborhoods. Together, they sponsor beautification projects and pay for overtime police protection for the neighborhood. FPA secured two vacant firehouses for a church and another community organization, which run youth programs and family services in them. It worked with more than fifty agencies and organizations to help a local pastor close a crack alley and convert it into a community garden, which drove down crime in the area by more than 13 percent in a few short months. The litany of activity continues.

FPA never focused its activities on a single set of issues. Instead, it stood ready to assist FBOs in carrying out initiatives in their communities in whatever way it could. It connected police with churches, neighborhoods to government agencies, and congregations to foundations that would not have otherwise considered funding them. Its impact has been widely felt, however, in several key areas. It has helped convert physical liabilities (such as crack houses and alleys) into community assets. It has strengthened public safety through increased congregational involvement in crime-fighting, with notable results. It has enabled more organizations to run more programs to serve more inner-city youth, and it has, in general, assisted a considerable number of small organizations—mainly FBOs—secure funding that they could not have secured on their own.[28]

The experience of FPA has not been replicated to the same degree and scale anywhere else. For this reason, it stands alone as a fascinating case study, the scope of which is beyond this book's present purposes. For now, it is worth looking at a few key principles gathered from interviews with its directors, staff, and FBO leaders in Indianapolis about what did and did not work to make FPA succeed in its mission.

Create effective partnerships. FPA staff regarded their main job to be responding to the communities' needs by bringing together other organizations and resources as quickly and effectively as possible. This works. This works well, in fact. Organizations sense that they are being empowered when they see their government working quickly to strengthen them beyond what they could do alone. Many positive "unintended consequences" have resulted from bringing community leaders together who had not previously worked in partnership.

Deliver quality customer service. FPA's success and high level of community respect has not only been a function of its ability to create solid partnerships. Its response time and capacity to get organizations on a fasttrack through the usual (and expected) government bureaucracy created high trust levels. This was the most important element in FPA's beginning, because many community-based organizations were initially skeptical of government's offer to help them. FPA built up trust by responding quickly to requests from FBO leaders—so much so, that it became standard practice for pastors and other leaders to regularly invite FPA "to the table" whenever key community issues were at stake.

Become a household name. FPA's ability to raise public awareness about the good work of Indianapolis' community-building groups through public events, press conferences, and weekly faxes raised the general public consciousness about its work. Goldsmith regularly used the bully pulpit—that is, his position as mayor to draw attention to projects being carried out in the community by churches and other organizations. This has, in turn, given FPA positive press and made Indianapolis residents familiar with its role in the community.

Call for help. Because of its unique vantage point in the mayor's office, FPA was often aware of underserved needs in the community. In situations such as these, it would then invite pastors and other faith leaders to address these needs and offer technical assistance and other resources to help. Instead of announcing yet another program to deal with a given issue, in this case government recognizes that the groups able to address a need should be asked to help—without being forced to do so. Because of the success Indianapolis churches have had in caring for teen parents, youth from the probation department, people unable to hold down jobs, and even city parks' landscaping, they have often been approached by city hall to address related needs. As a result, a number of self-sustaining partnerships have been created in the community between organizations that formerly were unfamiliar with each other's work but which joined hands to deliver a service or solve a problem when FPA brought them together.

Enable groups without creating dependency. In its intention to help, it was easy for FPA to do work for local groups that would eventually grow dependent upon FPA. For example, FPA staff regularly assisted organizations with grant applications, and because government staff are accustomed to the writing style required by application processes, it becomes too easy to assume a bulk of the writing load. But if a church or neighborhood organization does not learn how to secure grant monies itself, then FPA, or any other similar agency, is not truly working as an "enabler" of the organization.

Situate responsibility in the neighborhoods. As a coordinator of activity, FPA could not reasonably spearhead the activities that resulted from partnerships it helped to form. It is important that initiatives in neighborhoods be driven as much as possible by the groups in the neighborhoods. FPA existed to support the work that community-building institutions are doing and would have overstepped its self-appointed limits of authority by telling organizations what to do and how to do it. Community renewal happens when people out in the communities claim ownership for the change they want to have in their neighborhoods.

Liberals and conservatives, both within Indianapolis and across the nation, found great value in FPA as an idea and as a reality. Not only has it been heralded as innovative by a number of observers, it has been widely recognized as a good investment. It leveraged considerable amounts of activity with a rather limited budget. Also, by its mere existence and activity, it drew attention to the way in which religion can successfully occupy a corner in the public square without compromising its own character or that of government. Isaac Randolph, former director of FPA and currently executive director of the Indianapolis Ten Point Coalition, says that this is merely a picture of government doing what it has historically done best:

> *Throughout history, government has convened key groups and individuals to solve problems, leveraged resources to get the job done, and publicly highlighted—through speeches, proclamations, and documents—principles, practices, and values without which a people cannot flourish. These three functions have been at the heart of what we did in all Front Porch Alliance activity. Wherever the interests of government and faith overlap, whether it is housing or public safety or something else, it*

CHAPTER THREE

does not make sense for government to huddle in its own corner and try to fix problems that everyone knows it cannot fix by itself—problems rooted in the matters of the heart and soul.

Post-Welfare Reform and a Strong Civic Infrastructure

Recalling the example of sixteenth-century Emden, Germany, presented at the opening of Chapter One, we remember that its brilliance was in the way it broadened the work of charity to include additional members of the community and required those who were poor to work hard at not being poor anymore. The previous chapter looked at the unconventional inclusion of the marketplace in social welfare. The current chapter has focused upon the inclusion of agents of social change in a public square that has been too narrowly defined in recent decades by government programs. In both the Good Samaritan and FPA examples, people needing help have been better served than they would have if these programs had not been undertaken. The more that government can creatively involve other members of the community in the overall effort to improve the situation of the poor, the more the effort is *shared* and thereby owned by a larger group of stakeholders.

The growing movement to include local FBOs in public social initiatives is one example of this devolutionary tendency toward shared responsibility. This chapter, it is hoped, shows that broadening FBO participation can take multiple forms through the use of an intermediary. Intermediaries, in general, (1) represent the kind of organizational culture government is used to dealing with, while (2) at the same time they understand the culture of—and can relate to—FBOs in a way government cannot. In summary, they provide several distinct advantages:

They help expand the community of care without requiring FBOs to receive public funds. Though direct funding of FBOs is legitimate in a number of governmental programs, it is not the only—nor the best—way to engage them. It should be obvious to anyone that such partnerships may invite—though they do not necessitate—infractions of the First Amendment. The conditions for FBO usage of public funds set forth in the Charitable Choice clause admit of some ambiguity. The two case studies presented in this chapter demonstrate ways in which the strength of FBOs can be leveraged for social good with minimal transaction of public monies into the hands of the faith groups. In the case of Good Samaritan, no public funds go to any of the participating churches. Good Samaritan, itself an FBO, maintains a trusted and respected standing in the eyes of local public officials and presents no constitutional threat in its practices. And because of its established relationships with many local FBOs, it was able to expand the community of care much more effectively and quickly than if government officials had tried to do so on their own. In the case of the Front Porch Alliance, public monies were transferred to FBOs only in a very limited way and for publicly valid uses. For the most part, FPA avoided direct funding but leveraged other forms of resources to assist FBOs in their community-redeeming work. Beyond the important issue of constitutional integrity, Good Samaritan and FPA are leading examples of what seems to be a desired form of government-faith collaboration in America today. As stated earlier, nearly half the government–FBO collaborations in a recent study were not directly financial relationships.

They assist FBOs with gaps in capacity so that the FBOs can concentrate upon the work they do best. In both cases presented here the intermediary provides the administration of the relationship with a government office or agency, coordinates general program activity, and helps the FBOs position themselves as effective service providers. Good Samaritan is more "issue-focused" than FPA was. That is to say, Good Samaritan rallies churches around the project of helping people move from welfare to independence. FPA supported a range of activity, largely determined by the FBOs it served. In both cases, however, the FBOs do not work directly with the government agency (the county welfare agency, in the Good Samaritan example) or office (the mayor's office, in the FPA example). Both cases demonstrate the ways in which intermediaries "save" FBOs a lot of time and energy. Whether this takes the form of managing a government contract or connecting FBOs to other public and private resources and programs to which they previously had no access, the FBOs then become free to utilize their usually scarce resources directly on serving the people they have committed themselves to help. Intermediaries can truly leverage the strength of FBOs by playing this important role. This is not to say that administrative and operational capacity should not be built up wherever possible among FBOs. But capacity should not be "forced" unnecessarily, either.

They make it more difficult to "use" FBOs. Leaders in the faith community hold diverse opinions on the issue of government-faith collaboration, but one is hard-pressed to find any who think their work would be improved by letting government officials tell them what to do. Even those favorable to partnering their organizations with public agencies hold reservations about how much control government will seek to acquire over them. Accounts of how government contracting has secularized the mission and practice of several FBOs have been widely circulated and support faith leaders' concerns about a relationship with government.[29] And if examples of secularization are not enough to invoke a steady caution, the seemingly increasing use of references to God and religion by politicians suggests that FBOs stand a good chance of being politicized, that is, used for political ends.[30] When a 2000 presidential campaign adviser remarked that her party was "going to take back God this time," journalists of divergent political viewpoints reported the remark as an offensive politicization of faith, if not a downright sacrilegious statement. But it essentially passed without much of a public outcry. Small FBOs know that the capacity of the politically powerful to blithely regard them in terms of their political utility alone presents a sizable danger.

Intermediaries, such as those exemplified in this chapter, serve as a buffer between public agencies and smaller, independent FBOs. Their leaders generally regard themselves as servants of the FBOs as much as partners with a public organization. They offer FBOs the opportunity to be involved in a public effort to help people in need without being under the direct control of a public agency or coercive public officials.

This chapter has focused mainly upon well-kept souls as an important objective of any civic infrastructure. For communities that have made well-kept houses and well-kept bodies a priority, the case studies presented in this chapter represent practices that can be replicated in a way that rounds out any partially existing infrastructure. Of course, CDCs, performance contracting, and FBO engagement do not exhaust the possibilities for constructing a healthy civic infrastructure. But they do represent the best of recent emerging practices and trends.

A 1997 study published by the Urban Institute and funded by the Casey and Rockefeller Foundations and the U.S. Department of Housing and Urban Development reports that "community building" has broadened into a movement that is now attracting significant policy attention. Community building, the authors claim, is a movement toward greater local involvement in social problem-solving, higher levels of self-reliance, decreased levels of dependence upon government, and overall local renewal efforts in which local leaders and residents take a greater share of the ownership for policies and programs once mainly expected of government alone.[31] The authors regard the "most promising alternative" to past community-renewal efforts that relied either on distant national nonprofits or local government is "the establishment of *nongovernmental locally based intermediaries*." They focus attention upon the critical importance of CDCs, FBO s, and performance standards for social investment (though they do not specifically discuss performance contracting, as has been done here). They also recognize that no single agency or organization can take up sole responsibility for coordinating and carrying out a successful community-building effort. Community building requires civic infrastructure. Indeed, much of what the authors describe as community building is an investment in what has been described in this chapter as civic infrastructure. The trend toward decentralized and community-based solutions to social problems is in full force. The future success and strength of our civic infrastructure depends upon the ability of local and national leaders to coordinate activity in a way consistent with its decentralized and dynamic grassroots character.

It was said in the first chapter that welfare reform signaled the most dramatic movement within the social sector in recent times toward a devolutionary and multisector approach to helping people in need. Our post-welfare reform world requires shared responsibility for poverty among alternative and nontraditional community players. The diagram in Figure E brings together the case studies from Chapters Two and Three into pictorial form. Included in the diagram are several examples of single-sector programs and initiatives for comparison.

In our post-welfare reform environment successful strategies for transforming charity generally involve shared responsibility. The areas in Figure E created by overlapping circles do not merely represent programs and initiatives where two or more players are involved. Rather, they represent those efforts where there is *a shared mission*, however minimal. For example, ServiceMaster partners with social sector nonprofits primarily to expand business, not to engage in altruism. But the success of the social mission affects the success of its business. A mere relationship between multisector players may not indicate a shared mission. For instance, large social services contracts exist in many states across America between public agencies and for-profit service providers. While government, at least theoretically, has a vested interest in people leaving welfare for permanent self-sufficiency (namely so that they do not return for publicly funded services), large contractors often only have an interest in providing the minimum service to get paid. Such a relationship would not be fairly represented in Figure E where "Performance contracting" is inserted. Performance contracting differs in that it does not measure success in terms of, say, numbers of people placed in jobs alone. It also requires that a certain level of investment back into the community occur, and it encourages partnerships with smaller nonprofits and FBOs whose support provides people with what they need—not only to find a job but also to stay employed, advance in a career, and overcome debilitating personal problems.

Not only does the post-welfare environment work best when a mission is shared, it also works well whenever an absent sector is included in whatever way it can help. For instance, to stay with the performance contracting example, it can be safely said that the degree to which the contracting service provider can involve nonprofits and FBOs in providing needed human services,

Figure E

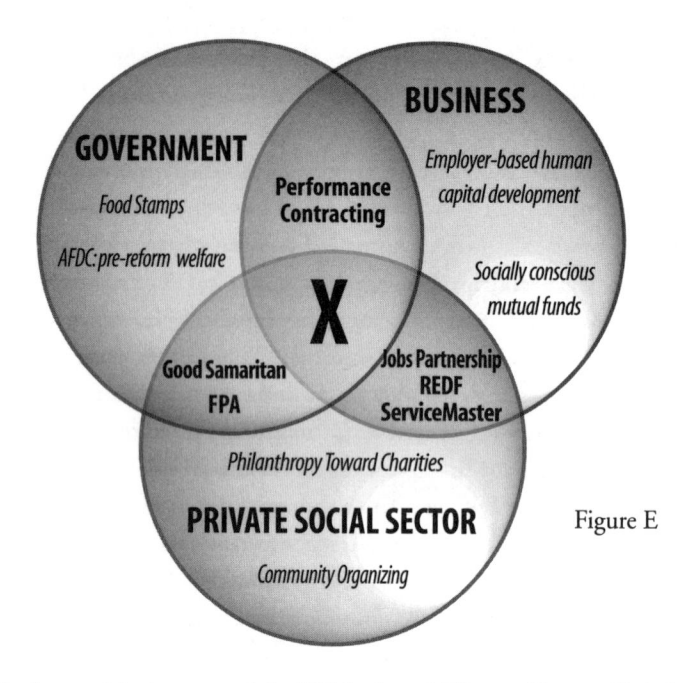

A Venn diagram with three overlapping circles labeled GOVERNMENT, BUSINESS, and PRIVATE SOCIAL SECTOR.

- GOVERNMENT only: Food Stamps; AFDC: pre-reform welfare
- BUSINESS only: Employer-based human capital development; Socially conscious mutual funds
- PRIVATE SOCIAL SECTOR only: Philanthropy Toward Charities; Community Organizing
- GOVERNMENT ∩ BUSINESS: Performance Contracting
- GOVERNMENT ∩ PRIVATE SOCIAL SECTOR: Good Samaritan; FPA
- BUSINESS ∩ PRIVATE SOCIAL SECTOR: Jobs Partnership; REDF; ServiceMaster
- Center (all three): X

the better. Moving toward the "X" in the middle would most likely benefit the community. Or in the case of Good Samaritan, increased participation of the business community as employment partners would only strengthen the community and provide enhanced help to the individuals and families moving from welfare to work. Moving toward the "X" may be a good strategy in this case.

Not every good program or initiative would be strengthened by adding an absent sector partner, however. "X" does not always mark the spot. In some cases an addition might hurt what is already running well. Each case requires individual consideration.

Figure E simply serves as a device for considering what kind of program actually exists and how it might be improved by multisector collaboration. "Philanthropy toward charities" in current practice works well as a purely private social sector activity. It may, in certain cases, be improved by working with a local government agency on a common problem or by incorpo-

CHAPTER THREE

rating market strategies. REDF, for example, does the latter. It may appear misleading to include REDF in the overlapping area between business and the social sector, since REDF is a foundation that invests in enterprises incorporated as nonprofits. However, this is just the point. The enterprises in REDF's portfolio actively work in the marketplace with paying customers and for-profit suppliers and partners. They do not generate surplus revenue that enriches shareholders. Rather, as nonprofits, they invest their profits back into their human services. But they are fully engaged in market activity and have for-profit partners that open opportunities for them. In another example, Aid to Families with Dependent Children (AFDC), or the old welfare system, existed as a government program with little to no shared mission with other sectors. One might regard its dissolution in 1996 as an attempt to move public social welfare toward the "X". Or, "Employer-based human capital development" that works with the local criminal justice system to recruit and provide training to ex-offenders in conjunction with church-supplied mentors would move toward the "X" and most likely result in an overall healthier community.[32]

There are no cut-and-dry policies that can create a multisector environment in a city or region. Most communities have multisector collaborations occurring all the time. The problem is that the majority of them happen in a terribly unsystematic way, or they are disconnected from any overarching effort to create a sustainable civic infrastructure. What local businesses, government, and social sector leaders can do is assess the condition of their community through the lens of a diagram such as that in Figure E. A fundamental question they might ask is, What problems could be addressed more effectively if responsibility for them was shared by entities from two or more sectors? And why are these entities currently not working together? The answers given to these two simple questions would frame a future civic-infrastructure-building initiative.

The answer given to the second question, in particular, will expose certain problems that do in fact affect policy. In some cases, in which public funds are involved, multisector collaborations are impeded by the "silo funding" that is characteristic of government funding scenarios. That is, much government funding for programs is targeted in a very specific way for very specific outcomes. This makes it difficult to engage in creative solutions at the local level. Cities and counties would be better served by general block grants than myriad funding streams that not only overstipulate the use of the dollars but also instigate much uncoordinated activity under numerous government programs. Block grants give wide discretion to local leaders in the use of the funds. Examples include Temporary Assistance to Needy Families (TANF) created by the welfare reform act and usable for countless strategies to help reduce poverty, and Community Development Block Grants, which local government officials can distribute for a broad range of community-building activities.

The main complaint with block grants is that they do not provide adequate protection against misuse. They offer too little guarantee that local leaders will use them in ways that truly benefit the community, their critics maintain. This brings us to another critical domain for policy makers. Rather than stipulating the specific kinds of programs and processes it wants to fund, government grants should base accountability on *real performance standards*. Government contracts at all levels—federal, state, local—are notoriously preoccupied with processes and "hollow outcomes" (for example, numbers of people served, units of housing built, and so on). Hollow outcomes do not tell us whether or not we have successfully addressed the core cause of a problem. Wherever funding is made more flexible by converting it into block grants, it should be accompanied by clear performance standards that focus upon demonstrable improvement in the situation of those individuals, neighborhoods, and communities the grants are deployed to serve. The best work in creating these standards, which is featured in the next chapter, is ridiculously underappreciated among policy makers, public officials, and the private sector alike. Many people roundly complain of government's waste of taxpayers' money on unproductive programs, but too few have recognized that entirely different assessment standards and tools are required than are currently used.

CHAPTER THREE

Endnotes

1 William Ryan, "The New Landscape for Nonprofits," *Harvard Business Review* (January-February 1999), 129.
2 Local Initiative Support Corporation, 1999 Annual Report.
3 The best recent account of the impact of CDCs is Paul Grogan and Tony Proscio, *Comeback Cities: A Blueprint for Urban Neighborhood Revival* (Boulder, CO: Westview Press, 2000), esp. 63–101.
4 For instance, the federal government only delivers about 4 percent of the programs it pays for (William Bennett and John DiIulio, "What Good Is Government?" *Commentary*, vol. 104, no. 5 [November 1997], 25). State and local governments naturally deliver a greater proportion of services, but they are accustomed to contracting with large national firms such as Lockheed-Martin and Maximus, for instance, to deliver social services.
5 Amy Sherman. *The Growing Impact of Charitable Choice: A Catalogue of New Collaborations Between Government and Faith-Based Organizations in Nine States* (Washington, D.C.: The Center for Public Justice, 2000), 15. In the 125 government partnerships involving several hundred FBOs in her study, Amy Sherman discovered that the church-state issue was, as she says, a "non-issue" for almost all people involved. At the local level trust had been generated between public officials and FBOs, and they had usually reached some sort of agreement—both official and unofficial—about how the FBOs' religious character would and could be expressed.
6 See, for instance, André Mizell's Rising Above *Poverty: The Consequences of Poverty Status and Individual Characteristics on Earnings* (Joint Center for Poverty Research Working Paper 106, Northwestern University and University of Chicago, 1999) uses the NLSY to focus on factors affecting the future earning power of poor young adults. Mizell's findings suggest rather clearly that aspirations and self-esteem are fundamentally related to future earning power, i.e., the lower one's aspirations and esteem, the lower one's future earnings. He also found that increasing the hours worked in a week positively impacts future earning levels.
7 Figure B is taken from David Ellwood's "The Plight of the Working Poor" (Brookings Institution Roundtable, 1999) and adapted from data contained in the 1998 Congressional Budget Office report, *Policy Changes Affecting Mandatory Spending for Low-Income Workers Not Receiving Cash Welfare*.
8 I refer primarily to the work of David Larson of the National Institute for Healthcare Research (referenced in Chapter Two's note seven), which has shown

TRANSFORMING CHARITY

so convincingly that religious commitment improves overall health according to a number of variables, that medical schools now offer instruction on the topic. For an overview of research confirming this thesis across a number of variables, see "Religion: The Forgotten Factor in Health Care," *The World and I,* vol. 11, no. 2 (February 1996), 292 ff.

9 The first study, authored by David Larson and Byron Johnson (New York: The Jeremiah Project Report 98-2, 1998), and modeled—as the title implies—on Larson's medical research cited earlier, is actually comprised of four studies that (1) reviewed over four hundred other studies between 1980 and 1997 that included religiosity as a variable in juvenile delinquency cases, (2) looked at the role of churchgoing on young black males in distressed communities, (3) examined the role of African-American churches in reducing delinquency in distressed communities, and (4) examined the effects of religiosity on a national sample of youth. The second study, which is the most recent, is published by the Center for Research on Religion and Urban Civil Society at the University of Pennsylvania (Report 2000-2).

10 Hodgkinson, Weitzman, & Kirsch, *From Belief to Commitment: The Community Service Activities and Finances of Religious Congregations in the United States: Findings from a National Survey* (Washington DC: Independent Sector, 1988), 51, emphasis added.

11 A new survey would have to account for the recent continued growth in areas of faith-based involvement such as affordable housing and crime reduction. With regard to affordable housing, for instance, the Fannie Mae Foundation claims that faith-based community development corporations have produced nearly 110,000 units of affordable housing in America, churches and other FBOs have produced 215,000 units for the elderly under the federal Section 202 program, and Habitat for Humanity another 350,000 (PR Newswire, April 7, 2000).

12 Sherman, 14.

13 See Ram Cnaan, Robert Wineburg, and Stephanie Boddie, *The Newer Deal: Social Work and Religion in Partnership* (New York: Columbia University Press, 1999), esp. 47–68.

14 On this point, a forward-looking research agenda can be found in *Religion and the Public Square* (ed. Ryan Streeter [Indianapolis: Hudson Institute, 2001]), the proceedings from an April 25–26, 2000, Wingspread conference, "The Future of Government Partnerships with the Faith Community," which drew together twenty-five practitioners, academics, and public officials to draft recommendations for the future of FBOs' interaction with the public sector.

15 Speech at the White House Prayer Breakfast, September 28, 1999 (Washington, D.C.: Federal Document Clearing House, 1999).

CHAPTER THREE

16 E. J. Dionne, "The Third Stage: New Frontiers in Religious Liberty," in Dionne and DiIulio, eds., *What's God Got to Do with the American Experiment* (Washington, D.C.: Brookings, 2000), 115–120, and "Religion and the Future of the American Experiment," American Outlook (Summer 2000), 26–28.

17 For an accounting of this trend, see Carl Esbeck, "A Constitutional Case for Governmental Cooperation with Faith-Based Social Service Providers," *Emory Law Journal* 46 (1997), 1, and Stephen Monsma, "Substantive Neutrality as a Basis for Free Exercise-No Establishment Common Ground," *The Journal of Church and State* 42 (Winter 2000), 13, and in the same issue, Abigail Lawlis Kuzma, "Faith-Based Providers Partnering with Government," esp. 58–67.

18 Researcher Mark Chaves has discovered in his National Congregations Study that churches in poor urban neighborhoods offer more social services than those in high-income neighborhoods, and within those neighborhoods, churches that have a greater amount of resources (usually because their members commute from higher-income neighborhoods) offer more social services. See Mark Chaves, *Congregations' Social Service Activities,* Urban Institute Briefing Paper 6 (Washington, D.C.: December 1999), 3.

19 "Religion and Public Life," *Brookings Review* (Spring 1999), 41.

20 Exclusion is currently a real problem. Both Amy Sherman and Center for Public Justice researcher Stanley Carlson-Thies report that their extensive involvement with state faith-based initiatives has revealed widespread systematic exclusion of legitimate FBOs from consideration as service providers. The exclusion may not be intentional but is still structural from the simple fact that these officials have never been involved with FBOs and do not know their own community-based landscape. They may instinctively turn to a large, well-known FBO with an invitation to bid on a contract without realizing that smaller—and sometimes more effective—FBOs exist in their community and would make impressive candidates.

21 These figures are from Mark Chaves, *Congregations' Social Service Activities,* (Urban Institute, Center on Nonprofits and Philanthropy, Policy Brief No. 6, 1999), 3, and remarks he made during the panel presentation, "The Faith Community and Welfare Reform," at the U.S. Department of Health and Human Services conference, "Welfare Reform and the Faith Community," New Orleans, Louisiana, November 16–17, 1999.

22 Karen Paciero Celinske, *Project Zero Data Management Report: One Year after Implementation* (State of Michigan Family Independence Agency Outstate Operations, 1997), 15–17.

23 Ibid., 24.

24 Ibid., 25.

25 Independent Sector arrives at its estimate by taking the nonagricultural hourly wage, as determined by the Economic Report of the President, and multiplying it by 12 percent for fringe benefits. I have calculated the value of volunteer hours during the course of Good Samaritan's contract by using an hourly wage of $14.03, which is the mean value between the 1996 and 1999 wages, as determined by Independent Sector's "Giving and Volunteering in the United States" (Washington: 1999).

26 Olgen Williams, "Caring for Our Civic Souls, *Blueprint Magazine,* Spring 1999.

27 Stephen Goldsmith, "Having Faith in Our Neighborhoods: The Front Porch Alliance," *What's God Got to Do with the American Experiment,* 76–77.

28 This information is treated more comprehensively in the forthcoming *Empowerment and the City: Citizen Engagement in Indianapolis, 1992–1999,* by Stephen Goldsmith (Indianapolis: Hudson Institute, 2001).

29 See, for example, Daniel T. Oliver and Vernon L. Kirby, "Catholic Charities: Mired in the Great Society?" *Alternatives in Philanthropy* (Washington, D.C.: Capital Research Center, February 1998), and Daniel T. Oliver, "Volunteers of America: From Christian Ministry to Government Contractor," *Alternatives in Philanthropy* (Washington, D.C.: Capital Research Center, August 1999). See also Joe Loconte's *Seducing the Samaritan: How Government Contracts Are Reshaping Social Services,* Pioneer Paper No. 13 (Boston: Pioneer Institute, 1997).

30 For a provocative account of this trend, see Jonathan Rauch's "McGod Bless America," *The National Journal,* vol. 31, no. 26 (June 26, 1999), 1869 (Rauch, a self-described atheist, is one example of a journalist who cites the following statement unflatteringly).

31 G. Thomas Kingsley, Joseph B. McNeely, and James O. Gibson, *Community Building: Coming of Age* (Washington, D.C.: Urban Institute, 2000).

32 My thanks to Jay Hein for first giving me the idea to use the Venn diagram in the manner employed here.

CHAPTER FOUR
Toward a High-Impact Social Sector

Social Spending in America

The premise of this book is that assistance to poor individuals and families is undergoing a transformation in America. Society's obligation to the poor is falling less upon the shoulders of government alone and more upon those of multisector networks. Federal, state, and local governments' increasing reliance on nongovernmental, local organizations is more than an attempt to "do more with less"—it is a recognition that relief for the poor should help transform lives from a status of dependency to independence. Governments, or at least reformers within governments, would prefer to turn consumers of tax-funded services into taxpayers (crudely put, but bluntly true). And many nonprofit human services providers, especially faith-based organizations (FBOs), are focusing their charitable missions on the kind of assistance that helps people overcome barriers to economic, emotional, and social well-being. We expect more of our human services institutions today. We want them to produce results. We are less and less satisfied with intention-based charity and want investment-based charity in its place.

Or so it seems. The United States social sector, including publicly and privately funded and operated organizations and programs, is massive. It is not, however, evaluated or assessed in a way that reflects its size and scope. Remarkably, there exists hardly any consistency in America on the question

TRANSFORMING CHARITY

of how to assess the impact of the social sector so that we might invest in it more prudently.

The nonprofit sector in America consists of more than 1.14 million organizations with annual revenues of $621.4 billion.[1] This represents 6.2 percent of the nation's economy, and it is larger than the individual gross national product (GNP) of ten of the fifteen European Union member nations.[2] Human services organizations in the United States, excluding health services, represent approximately $50 billion, or roughly 8 percent, of total nonprofit spending. Including health services, human services account for more than half the total.[3] The nonprofit sector employs 10.2 million people, or 6.9 percent of America's workforce, and it grew 25 percent in the 1990s. The IRS received 80,000 applications for nonprofit status in fiscal year 2000 and reportedly has a $137 million budget for reviewing and auditing them.[4]

Federal spending on human services accounts for nearly 12 percent of America's GDP. More than $440 billion is spent annually by the U.S. Departments of Housing and Urban Development, Health and Human Services, and Labor, which are responsible for housing, health, employment, welfare and general community services for poor Americans. The three agencies employ nearly 100,000 people.[5] Among federal agencies, only the U.S. Treasury has greater outlays than the Department of Health and Human Services ($385 billion compared to $375.5 billion). The Department of Defense trails them both by more than $100 billion.[6]

It is difficult to calculate the total dollar value of the social sector. Total federal spending in the sector, including services such as crime prevention and education but excluding Social Security, amounts to approximately $500 billion annually. Combined with the nonprofit social sector, this figure jumps to well over $1 trillion—larger than the combined economies of Canada and Mexico. This does not even include the amount of money spent by state and local governments on social sector activity. Considered as a whole, America's social sector spending likely exceeds every EU member's GNP, with the exception of Germany.

CHAPTER FOUR

In spite of the tremendous size of social sector spending over against our total economy, we do not currently have generally accepted methods or metrics for assessing the socioeconomic impact of our human services. Some social sector programs are admittedly too difficult to measure. But many are not, and better accountability (and accounting) practices would enable a much greater understanding of where our charitable and other human services spending is taking us. How much does the taxpayer save when someone moves successfully from welfare to work? And if we could calculate this, what policies could be designed so that local communities truly receive the benefit of the savings? How much does the person who has moved from welfare to work benefit economically from the service provided? What is the collective benefit to a local economy from the efforts of its public and private organizations whose job it is to move people into economic self-sufficiency? If we cannot answer questions such as these, how can we *really* know how well these organizations are using the resources available to them?

The absence now of reliable indicators for social sector investment means a greater potential for poor performance later. On top of currently growing social-sector spending sits the immense wealth to be inherited by the next several generations, referenced in Chapter One. Paul Schervish, regarded as America's foremost expert on intergenerational wealth transfers, and John Havens, say that their "low-range best estimate is that over the 55-year period from 1998 to 2052 the wealth transfer will be $41 trillion, and may well reach double or triple that amount."[7] They estimate that the transfer could reach $136 trillion. A sizable portion of this wealth (conservatively estimated at $6 trillion) will be available for social sector investment as the inheritors seek tax advantages and pursue their particular philanthropic interests. While no single organization or agency should be given the privilege of determining how and where that money is philanthropically invested, it is a shame that we can offer future philanthropists no better indication of how well their money is working than simple cost-benefit analysis or occasional anecdotes.

Social Investment in America

Renowned Harvard business professor, Michael Porter, together with Mark Kramer, writes about the giving practices of American foundations: "Little effort is devoted to measuring results. On the contrary, foundations often consider measuring performance to be unrelated to their charitable mission. If foundations are to survive and thrive in the new century, those attitudes and practices must change."[8] In order to overcome these rather unhelpful "attitudes and practices," foundations should concentrate on "creating value," Porter and Kramer say. These attitudes and practices reflect a notion of charity in which intentions ("charitable mission") are prioritized over investments and could just as easily be used to describe the giving practices of many American individuals or government social spending in general.

In our current world of transforming charity, expectations are beginning to change, and more and more people are expecting greater and greater evidence that our social spending is achieving the best possible results. We know how to assess the way that value is created in our capital markets, and now we want to know what it means to create value through our charitable and social spending. Almost daily, articles appear in newspapers and magazines describing the felt need to have better tools for measuring the return on our social investments. For example, in a recent *Time* magazine article, John Doerr, founder of the $20 million New Schools Ventures Fund, a foundation dedicated to investing in educational issues by raising capital from venture capitalists and CEOs, asks, "How will we, or a third party, measure how this works?" *Time* says that Doerr "would like to see some rugged capitalism applied to weed out inefficient organizations so that more money would flow to those that are really maximizing their results."[9] A recent article in *Governing* magazine on the Local Initiative Support Corporation, which invests in neighborhood revitalization, reports that a local community development corporation is "trying to develop new measures that will track success in the softer areas" such as "housing values, crime statistics, school delinquency, and residents' net worth."[10]

These are only current examples of an emerging trend that can be found in literature on philanthropy and government spending, which continues to raise the question, how do we measure the return on social investments? Rarely, however, does one find any answers to the question.

Value can be created in numerous ways in the social sector, and the manner in which one defines social value will determine the manner in which one assesses how successful a social investment is. From their analysis of foundation activity, Porter and Kramer see four ways that value is created. Foundations can create value, they say, by funding the best and most efficient grantees, attracting additional investment from other donors to the charitable cause or organization they are funding, improving the performance of the grantee, and most important, advancing the knowledge of a field by paying for research.[11] Another Harvard scholar, Peter Frumkin, has also examined the domains in which philanthropic activity can be evaluated for real impact. Like Porter and Kramer, he holds that adding to knowledge and building organizational capacity are ways of creating value. He also claims that impact can be assessed to the degree that philanthropy enriches the lives of clients served by a particular program or organization, creates social capital by encouraging various groups within a community to work together in new ways to solve problems, and expresses the values and beliefs of the philanthropist.[12]

Each of the preceding three chapters has referenced the need for a wiser, more robust notion of "investment" in our institutions designed to serve the poor. Without a well-articulated notion of investment and value-creation, it is impossible to articulate a feasible notion of "return on investment" for the hundreds of billions of dollars that we spend trying to fix social problems every year. If we were able to articulate the value created in the social sector according to a "composite index" formed from the domains of value creation given by Porter, Kramer, and Frumkin earlier, we would have a rich understanding of value indeed. It is highly unlikely that we will have anything like this soon. But it is likely that we will be able to determine the return on our investments in organizational capacity, the lives of the people receiving services, and the overall economic and social impact of services on the communities in which they are delivered, just as it is likely that we will make advances in the next decade in calculating the value of such activities as adding to knowledge or creating social capital.

Currently, the only domain of value creation receiving substantial attention is that of organizational capacity-building among nonprofit organizations and, to some extent, governmental agencies. As mentioned in the first chapter, for-profit consulting companies such as Boston-based Bain and Company, have created a new market niche by assisting nonprofits become more business-savvy. A number of online services for nonprofits are popping up that equip them with information, training skills, and networks to which they previously did not have access. And universities have begun to pay attention to the size and scope of the nonprofit sector and its need for better business management practices, improved revenue-generation strategies, and better strategic planning. Harvard University has gotten in front of this issue both through its Social Enterprise Initiative at its business school and the Hauser Center for Nonprofit Organizations. Stanford's business school has launched its Center for Social Innovation, which seeks to "promote more innovative, effective, and efficient solutions to social problems in the United States and around the world."[13] Other well-known universities have also made "social enterprise" a part of their business school offerings. In general the number of college and university programs in nonprofit management have increased significantly in the past ten years.[14]

This newfound interest in social sector capacity-building is not the result of the discovery of a lucrative business opportunity. After all, Bain and Company's consultants take a pay cut to work with nonprofits. Nor is it likely the result of an increased supply of altruism into the hearts of Americans. It is, rather, a reaction to the growing recognition that our "sectored society," neatly broken up into for-profit, not-for-profit, and governmental organizations, is a bit artificial, given the complex tasks and problems we face every day. Business decisions affect the social condition of a community. Welfare policy affects employers through restrictions it places on low-income labor markets. Building capacity in social purpose organizations can, and often does, affect the economic and social health of their communities. Severyn Bruyn's *Civil Economy: Transforming the Market in the Twenty-First Century* represents the first book-length treatment of the many ways in which our social purpose institutions and our market economy overlap, depend on one another, reinforce each other's activities, and even blur into one another.[15] Jed Emerson, whose metric for social return on investment is presented later, has produced a working paper as part of Harvard Business School's Social Enterprise Series that speculates on the need for and possibility of a "blended value proposition" in our assessments of financial and social returns on investment.[16] Publications such as these would probably have not been possible fifty years ago because the questions to which they respond were not being asked. But today, questions abound with respect to measuring the impact of our social sector. This should be no surprise, given the way in which the three main sectors of society—government, business, social or nonprofit—overlap in a world of transforming charity. The interests of charitable and other social institutions are interwoven with the interests of the other sectors like never before.

But building the capacity of nonprofit and other social purpose institutions to be more "businesslike" will not necessarily help us measure, or even define, results. It may help those institutions produce more of the "outcomes" they are in the business of producing, but we are still left with the question, Can we say that value has been created? And in order to answer this, we need to have more sophisticated ways of accounting for the full social and economic value that is created by socially redeeming activity. This will be addressed below, but first, we have to take seriously the possible objection that might be raised at this point: *Why* should we ultimately care about measuring the return on our social investments? Just because more and more people are suggesting that we should assess results does not automatically mean that it is a good idea. Why not just let our social sector activity continue in its current form? After all, it achieves immeasurable good, and it should stay that way—that is, it should remain immeasurable. This is a reasonable objection.

There are five main reasons why we should have a better way of measuring the impact, or return on investment (ROI), of human services.

1. *Measuring ROI will enable us to truly see who is creating the most value.* Small community-based organizations should not fear this kind of assessment but should rather embrace it. It may be what proves their work to be more effective, dollar-for-dollar, than the larger, well-connected nonprofit organizations that know how to respond to government requests-for-proposal, have training budgets, and appear to be having a massive impact because of the thousands of people they serve. Lester Salamon, a leading authority on nonprofit organizations, has described a "crisis of effectiveness" plaguing nonprofits today: it is no longer assumed that they will do the good job serving people that was once expected of them without question.[17] Measuring ROI would give us a better dollar-for-dollar sense of who is truly changing lives and helping people out of poverty and who is not—that is, who is truly the most effective.

2. *Without good measurement of returns, we have no way to combat the "we just need more money" argument.* ROI shifts the conversation about funding for human services away from how much money an organization says it needs to what is actually being done with the amount that it has. This revives the old idea of stewardship, which is inherently an idea about taking responsibility for creating positive change regardless of how much money or how many resources one has. Currently, social service organizations and agencies justify their existence and need for additional funding by their stated intentions and the size of the problem they are trying to address ("there are x people needing job training, and we need y dollars to serve them"). ROI would enable us to see more clearly how much it costs to produce a desired result, thus giving us better grounding for decisions that concern how much to invest in a given program or organization.

3. *ROI would give us a metric around which to coordinate publicly funded social programs and determine acceptable results.* It is com-

mon knowledge that government agencies such as the Departments of Health and Human Services, Housing and Urban Development, and Labor have a variety of funding streams and programs that address similar issues but are often entirely disconnected from one another and sometimes in direct conflict with each other. This problem is made even more acute at local and state levels where additional layers of programs and regulations complicate matters and confuse officials who try to figure out which dollars can be used for which activities. A shared set of desired outcomes should fuel policy debates, and ROI is one way to determine what those outcomes should be. We want a solid return on the taxes we pay, and ROI applied to public policy could help eliminate the inexcusable waste generated by cross purposes, unclear performance standards, and the overall focus upon processes rather than results indicative of too many government programs. The thought that government can be "reinvented" without concentrated attention on ROI is perhaps one of the larger management oversights of the past decade.

4. *We should demand a lot from people helping people.* Public and private assistance to poor and low-income families is primarily about helping them, not just about creating jobs and job security for those who deliver the services. Many current forms of aid to the poor look exactly the opposite. ROI intensifies accountability within the social sector, and this should be embraced as a good thing. Better practices for assessing social "returns" would provide invaluable assistance to organizations helping the poor so that as many dollars are used as wisely as possible. Transforming charity is not only about the transformation of the lives of those receiving assistance. It is first and foremost about transforming the practices of those who claim to be providing help to the poor and other at-risk individuals and families. Low performance standards and unaccountable good intentions are

often accepted as routine for any form of public or private social work, but there is no universal law dictating that this be the case. It exists mainly due to the absence of any sound accountability mechanism such as that provided by ROI measures. Those who depend on services to help them escape poverty and other afflictions have the most to lose by our inattention to this issue. None of this should be construed to mean, however, that those working within the social sector should merely be scrutinized more heavily and be weighed down with more stress at work. A performance-driven social sector is likely to produce better and more appealing employment opportunities than it currently offers.

5. *Finally, the process of establishing commonly shared ROI standards is one way for us to have a publicly meaningful dialogue about what the goal of charity is.* Much of the current emphasis on nonprofit capacity-building, for instance, focuses on the means of delivering human services but leaves the ends out of the equation. This is fine to the extent that we simply want nonprofit organizations, no matter their cause or goal, to run more accountably and effectively. But if we are to truly understand the benefit of human services, we cannot proceed long without asking what is ultimately good for those we are serving. Some social purpose work is only good for some, and other kinds of services are good for all. There is a big difference between nonprofit or governmental efforts to stop smoking or to restrict the work of certain companies or industries for the sake of the environment, and services and programs that move someone from public assistance to productive self-sufficiency. In the former case, no matter the merits, someone loses, whether it is the tobacco company employee who loses his or her job or the rural residents of a town whose job prospects are ended because of a successful environmental effort to keep a large company away. In the latter case, it would be difficult to argue that anyone loses by having

someone begin the process of self-sufficiency, so long as that person is not thrown into a worse condition than if he or she were still reliant on public assistance. Should a coalition of foundations, service providers, representatives of government, and businesses come together to begin sketching out commonly accepted ROI standards, they would likely force the question of how our services benefit communities and society as a whole. This would be a good thing. And we may discover that a successful set of ROI standards and measures is only reliable in good-for-all scenarios. Good-for-some scenarios in which someone loses may be too complicated to generate a solid notion of value creation and thus, ROI.

In light of this last point, a fruitful process of establishing commonly shared ROI standards would do well to start in the domain of services to the poor and low-income families. Wherever we have committed massive amounts of public funding and programming in the social sector usually indicates an area about which most Americans have some concern. No one wants poverty and crime in their communities. If we have committed public resources to address these problems, then we can usually measure success not only by their diminishment but also by diminished future need for spending in these areas. This is one place to start.

Measuring Return on Investment

We are not entirely without guidance when it comes to beginning the process of measuring ROI for programs aimed at moving people out of poverty and into independence. The two best current examples of ROI applied to such programs are by no means mainstream or executed by any of the large, well-established performance management firms or agencies. Each is relatively small in its current scope and is forward-looking in its practice and ambition. One is currently being used in the public sector and the other in the private sector.

The first example is found in the work of Dennis Benson's *Return on Inve$tment: Guidelines to Determine Workforce Development Impact*. Geared primarily for publicly funded workforce development programs (such as the former Job Training Partnership Act and the current Workforce Investment Act programs), Benson's work takes into account the taxes "saved" by such programs, the economic benefit to the clients of the programs, and the overall economic benefit of the programs to the local economy. In other words, it is a way of understanding the positive changes in people's lives in terms of the economic value they create.

The ROI models that Benson has created are thus primarily financial calculations in their focus upon reduced public expenditures, increased client earnings, and so on. However, once they are applied to actual programs, the figures they generate in turn generate questions such as, "What kind of service was provided that enabled Agency A to get such a higher return than Agency B?" To answer questions such as these, we would then look at (1) the difference in method and style for delivering services and (2) the characteristics of the populations served by the programs. If one of the service providers made use of an extensive network of grassroots, faith-based organizations that provided mentors for program participants, this difference would be important in informing our decisions about the differences in the ROIs between the two organizations. And if one of the providers served, for instance, a disproportionately high number of drug-addicted clients, this would have to be figured into the assessment of the differences. Hopefully, in the long run, a "risk factor" based on different populations will be available for incorporation into the overall ROI calculation. But no reliably tested risk model currently exists.

In any case, it should be evident that an ROI analysis helps us see the economic value of changes in people's lives. A basic cost-benefit analysis is primarily an economic view of an organization and does not necessarily make a connection between the dollars invested and the changes in people's lives. And an account of the purely social benefits of a program, such as improved relationships between mothers in the program and their children, is quite difficult to measure. But the ROI models that Benson has developed (primarily through his work as a consultant to publicly funded agencies) enable us to measure the socioeconomic benefit of "social investments."

ROI-T

Benson refers to the reduced reliance on public expenditures as "Return on Investment to Taxpayers" (ROI-T). This is a metric calculated to determine the degree to which a service both reduces the public subsidies to support an individual and increases that individual's tax contributions. ROI-T is calculated by adding the reduction in public expenditures for the individuals served, their increased tax contributions, and their portion of FICA (Social Security).[18] Public expenditures can be "saved" only if someone formerly receiving them no longer receives them because of an intervention by a human services provider.

ROI-D

While a number of organizations calculate something approximating ROI-T as a way to "show results," it is only a part of Benson's overall ROI model. He refers to "Return on Investment—Disposable Income" (ROI-D) as a way to see whether or not the earnings of clients have increased over a given amount of time. Welfare reform has been praised as a success because the number of people on welfare has plummeted, but if we cannot show that the situations of those formerly on welfare have improved over a reasonable amount of time, we have arguably failed to impact poverty. Similarly, ROI-D is figured by subtracting the eliminated public expenditures, increased tax contributions, and client share of FICA from the increased earnings experienced as a result of the service provider's intervention.[19] Clients served by job training and other workforce services generally spend their disposable income in their local economy. Because of this, increasing their disposable income is in the interest of their communities. If they have less to spend than they did while on public assistance, not only are we ineffective in helping them to get ahead, but their community as a whole has less to gain as well. This latter point hardly ever factors into public policy considerations, though it should.

ROI-E

Benson's third metric concerns the ripple effect of a service in the local economy, "Return on Investment—Economic Impact" (ROI-E). He makes use of economic multipliers developed by the U.S. Department of Commerce to calculate the long-term economic impact of the people served by a program and of the program itself. It is beyond the purposes of this book to delve into the level of detail needed to understand the Department of Commerce's "regional multipliers." But they can be summarily understood as two tools, one that determines the overall benefit to the local economy from the total increase in the net income of people served by a particular program, and another that determines the economic benefit of running the program itself in a particular community. Together with the increased tax and FICA contributions, they generate ROI-E, which indicates the per-dollar value of the program as a whole to its community.

Benson then applies an additional multiplier to ROI-T, ROI-D, and ROI-E to generate their long-term impact within a community.[20] This is done to gain an understanding of the degree to which job training and placement services can be said to be an investment over time. So long as they are greater than the public funds required to provide the services over time, they can be said to be generating net positive economic "returns" to the taxpayers of the communities in which they are administered.[21]

There are, of course, greater complexities in calculating returns in this manner than can be accommodated here. Collecting data in a reliable and consistent way—so that the metrics can be accurately deployed—is always a challenge. Data available on clients before and after they leave organizations' services are often difficult to come by, especially in a way that helps rather than hinders the calculation process. The fact that public assistance can come in a variety of forms skews the process, and the fact that local public information systems are not coordinated well enough to give full and accurate information on clients also creates a barrier. Housing vouchers come from one agency, food stamps from somewhere else, and the individual receiving them goes to a job training program paid for by yet another place. Despite advances in "one-stop" centers in which low-income individuals can obtain multiple services, the coordination of information and the bulk of social welfare services has a long way to go. Also, Benson's model does not yet adequately incorporate the Earned Income Tax Credit (EITC), a large income assistance program for low-income, working families (recall Figure B in Chapter Three), mainly because his clients do not collect EITC data. It would need to be correctly factored into the ROI-D and ROI-T scenarios in order to generate an accurate picture of public expenditure versus increased earnings.

But none of this should overshadow the valuable contribution that Benson's work makes to the future of the social sector. He has provided an invaluable ROI model upon which a coherent, publicly valid system of ROI measurement could be built. He has applied his model to a variety of service providers around the nation, and others have begun to apply his model to their own organizations for internal assessment. But only when a comparative analysis is done in a geographic region between providers of similar services will we have an idea of how government investment should "look." If we analyze a single provider whose returns are greater than the taxpayer investment, this may not tell us anything so long as it stands alone. Only when we can see programs side-by-side and assess their returns in light of each other will we be able to make judgments about the value they have truly created. This has never been done and thus serves as a challenge to social sector leaders everywhere who at least say they are interested in improving results in human services.

Social Return on Investment—REDF Again

Chapter Two featured the Roberts Enterprise Development Fund (REDF) as an example of how the mission meets the market in a forward-looking, promising way. Beyond its venture-philanthropy method of capitalizing social purpose enterprises, REDF has developed the most sophisticated model of "social return on investment" (SROI) in the United States. Like Benson's work, REDF's SROI model has grown out of its actual experience applying it to real, live organizations. Unlike Benson's work, REDF's centers upon private organizations and thus gives the present chapter a well-

TRANSFORMING CHARITY

rounded perspective. As described in Chapter Two, REDF acts like a venture capitalist for 501(c)(3) enterprises that run businesses. It is thus in a strategic position to be able to apply its SROI analysis on the enterprises that it capitalizes.

Jed Emerson, former REDF executive director, and Jay Wachowicz, describe REDF's SROI analysis in the following way:

- It examines a social service activity over a given time frame (usually five to ten years).

- It calculates the amount of "investment" required to support that activity and analyzes the capital structure of the nonprofit that is in place to support that activity.

- It identifies the various cost savings, reductions in spending and related benefits that accrue as a result of that social service activity.

- It monetizes those cost savings and related benefits (that is to say, it calculates the economic value of those costs in real dollar terms).

- It discounts those savings back to the beginning of the investment time frame using a discounted cash flow analysis.

- And finally, it presents the socioeconomic value created during the investment time frame, expressing that value in terms of present value and SROI rates and ratios.[22]

REDF's SROI analysis is born of two guiding principles that get to the heart of value creation. First, according to Emerson and Wachowicz, a dollar invested in the mission of a socially redeeming organization may generate future economic and social returns in excess of that dollar's original value and can thus truly be called an investment. Second, many nonprofit organizations and other socially motivated enterprises create value that largely goes undocumented and is hardly appreciated.[23] The SROI analysis that REDF performs on its portfolio of nonprofit enterprises is part of a larger project to calculate the total value of those enterprises. Without an adequate metric for assessing the financial value of the enterprises' social benefits, REDF's portfolio value would be radically underassessed. In order to understand the value creation of a social purpose enterprise, one must add the economic value to the social benefit value.

When assessing the value of current portfolio enterprises, REDF analyzes its investment options in terms of the following factors:

1. Projected business performance: how much cash will the enterprise generate as a result of the investment?

2. Projected social benefits: how many new jobs will be secured for the target population served by the enterprise, what is the expected wage rate, and how much will be generated in taxes by those jobs?

3. Projected social welfare savings: how much will public expenditures be reduced in the target population, and what are the projected costs of serving the target population?[24]

The cash generated (number 1) is calculated like free cash flows in any for-profit enterprise valuation. This is the enterprise value. The social purpose value of the enterprise is calculated by subtracting the cost of serving the target population from the savings in public expenditures (number 3), and adding this amount to the new taxes paid by the target populations once they have been employed (number 2). The enterprise value and social purpose value are added together (less any debt) for the total value of the enterprise. In its investment assessment process, REDF forecasts these values ten years into the future, calculates a perpetuity based on year 10, and discounts them back to the present using a variety of discount rates. The present value of the enterprise and social purpose value is divided by the present value of the investment to date in the organization to calculate an Index of Return.

Emerson, the originator of REDF's SROI template, has interests that go well beyond the scope of the current chapter, not the least of which is the use of SROI analysis to determine share values of nonprofit organizations in a possible—yet still very hypothetical—nonprofit capital market.[25] While such a market is not nearly as speculative as it first sounds, and while it would add a much greater capacity than we have at present for philanthropists and other social sector investors to truly see the value they are helping create, one does not need to understand it—or even buy into it—to begin benefiting from REDF's SROI experiment. Several points are in order.

First, REDF's SROI analysis shows perhaps more clearly than any other assessment of nonprofit sector results how the mission and the market meet and relate. REDF is currently issuing its first SROI Reports, which provide clear indicators of socioeconomic impact and SROI values.[26] For instance, REDF's recent *SROI Report on Recycled Merchandise*, a social purpose enterprise of Bay Area nonprofit, Youth Industry, presents a detailed picture of the organization's social and economic value. Figure A shows a page from the report that breaks down the social purpose and enterprise financials.

The enterprise collects used merchandise for wholesale resale to thrift stores, employing 18- to 24-year-olds facing a range of barriers to future well-being and independence. The SROI Report combines hard financial data with key social impacts such as reduced homelessness and substance abuse. And then it assesses the combined value of the business and social benefit of the enterprise. Recycled Merchandise's enterprise value is nearly $2 million, and its social purpose value is more than $3 million. The per-dollar enterprise and social purpose Indices of Return are 14.48 and 24.97, respectively, for a Blended Index of Return of 39.45 (see Figure B). This means that for every dollar invested in the social purpose enterprise, fourteen dollars were generated by the enterprise (Enterprise Index of Return) and nearly twenty-five dollars in social savings to taxpayers and increased disposable income to clients were generated (Social Purpose Index of Return). The Blended Index of Return adds these two numbers together (adjusting for debt).

CHAPTER FOUR

SOCIAL PURPOSE RESULTS (PER TARGET EMPLOYEE)	1999
PUBLIC SAVINGS	$5,735
NEW TAXES	$2,133
WAGE IMPROVEMENT	$14,220
FINANCIAL IMPROVEMENT	$12,418

ENTERPRISE FINANCIALS	1998	1999	2000P
SALES	$1,024,112	$915,882	$1,058,067
GROSS MARGIN	80%	84%	82%
NET MARGIN (BEFORE S&S)[1]	15%	16%	10%
NET MARGIN (AFTER S&S)	16%	18%	11%

SOCIAL PURPOSE ENTERPRISE INDICATORS	1998	1999	2000P
TOTAL EMPLOYEES / TOTAL TARGET EMPLOYEES	39/34	23/17	25/21
FTE EMPLOYEES / FTE TARGET EMPLOYEES	6/4	8/5	9/6
SOCIAL OPERATING EXPENSES PER TARGET EMPLOYEE	$14	$28	$23

TOTAL PROJECTED INVESTMENT	$0
TOTAL PROJECTED SOCIAL SAVINGS AND NEW TAXES	$3,244,813
TOTAL PROJECTED SOCIAL OPERATING EXPENSES	$9,192
TOTAL PROJECTED CONTRIBUTION TO PARENT	$1,871,229

[1] S&S: Subsidies and Social Operating Expenses

REVENUES AND EXPENSES

	1998	1999	2000P
Social Subsidies	$17,000	$18,750	$10,000
Sales	$1,024,112	$915,882	$1,058,067
Social Operating Expenses	$480	$480	$480
Enterprise Expenses	$874,407	$770,560	$955,009

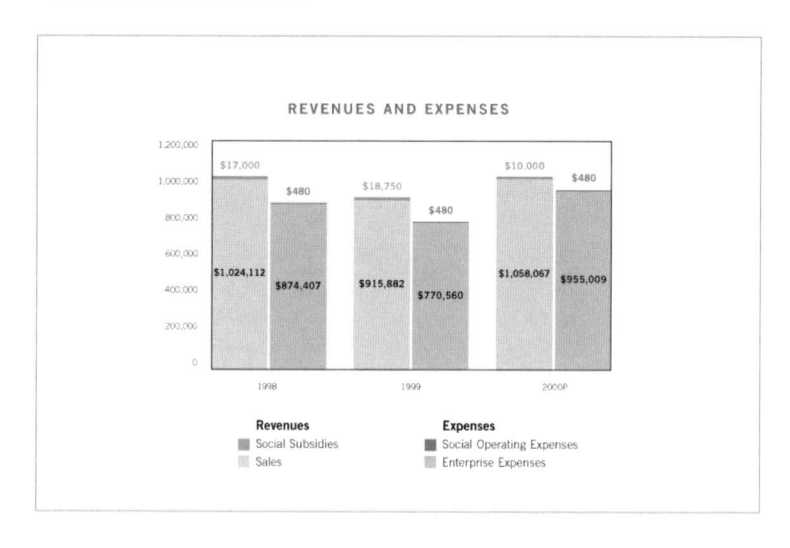

Figure A

TRANSFORMING CHARITY

SROI Report · Winter 2000

THE ROBERTS ENTERPRISE DEVELOPMENT FUND
a philanthropic venture of The Roberts Foundation

Recycled Merchandise
PARENT AGENCY: YOUTH INDUSTRY

BUSINESS SUMMARY: Recycled Merchandise is Youth Industry's social purpose enterprise that collects used clothing and household items and sells wholesale to Youth Industry's Nu2u & Nu2u2 enterprises and other Bay Area thrift stores.

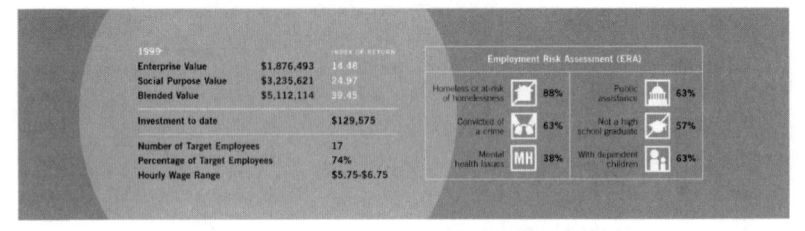

1999		INDEX OF RETURN
Enterprise Value	$1,876,493	14.48
Social Purpose Value	$3,235,621	24.97
Blended Value	$5,112,114	39.45
Investment to date	$129,575	
Number of Target Employees	17	
Percentage of Target Employees	74%	
Hourly Wage Range	$5.75-$6.75	

Employment Risk Assessment (ERA)

Homeless or at-risk of homelessness	88%	Public assistance	63%
Convicted of a crime	63%	Not a high school graduate	57%
Mental health issues	38%	With dependent children	63%

OVERVIEW

- Provides a professional environment for youth employees to experience the real demands of business and employers

- Youth exhibiting high motivation and capabilities can become Assistant-Managers-In-Training and learn supervising and inventory skills, as well as the daily opening and closing routine of the business

- On average, improves a target employee's income by $14,220 and saves the public $5,735 per target employee in public assistance and social service costs

TARGET EMPLOYEE STATISTICS

AVERAGE TIME WITH RECYCLED MERCHANDISE
3 months

AGE
50% 18-20 years old
50% 21-24 years old

RACE/ETHNICITY
63% Latino/a
37% African-American

GENDER
100% male

EMPLOYEE HIGHLIGHT

Raul joined the team at Youth Industry Recycled Merchandise (YIRM) when he decided that he wanted more out of life than the street had to offer. While employed at YIRM, Raul went from living in Golden Gate Park and abandoned vehicles to obtaining his own apartment. His performance on the job enabled him to become an Assistant-Manager-In-Training and supervisor of his peers. After setting a goal to become a driver for YIRM, Raul obtained his driver's license and began driving YIRM's Mitsubishi Fuso. It was not long before he was qualified to graduate from YI and accept a driving position with an organic produce company. His new boss called YI several times to commend Raul's performance. Raul has continued to volunteer with YI's Artist Mentorship Program, where he discovered his love for photography. He is now building on those skills and attending school to learn Web design.

Sales and Number of Target Employees

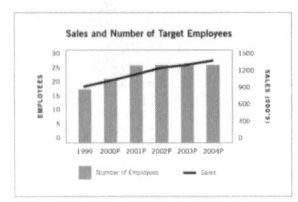

Figure B

CHAPTER FOUR

The SROI Reports have a "Key Social Impact Findings" section (Figure C), which shows (quite impressive) results and helps explain why the Social Purpose Index of Return is so high. With these economic and social indicators together in the same report, we begin to see linkages between investment strategies, the allocation of resources, and changed lives unlike ever before. Were SROI Reports used by a variety of organizations, we could compare those serving the same basic target population and then assess the SROI metrics side-by-side. Once a number of organizations besides REDF begin conducting this analysis regularly and in different localities, an entirely new culture of social sector valuation and assessment would take hold. And we could finally start being true to our rhetoric of investment in the social and charitable sector.

Second, REDF's analysis and that conducted by Benson combine to paint a picture of what the future of transformed charity could look like from a performance perspective. Both calculate the return taxpayers are getting because of a given service and the improvement in the earnings of those served. Benson's calculations more strongly emphasize the overall benefit to the local economy, and REDF's the real and projected value of the organization delivering the service. The metrics presented by the two together point us to soil rife with possibility for a new performance culture. When we consider the possibilities of these kinds of ROI analyses occurring on a larger scale, it becomes obvious that we are living in something of a social sector dark ages. Our ability to give an account of the way we manage resources that affect fragile, human lives is nowhere near where it should be, given our current technological capability and supposed concern for those lives. Higher standards of social sector performance are possible. The question is whether or not we have the will (or stomach) for them.

Third, REDF could not do what it does without a sizable investment in information technology. It has built an elaborate Management Information System (MIS) tracking system that receives social impact data from each of the organizations in its portfolio and those organizations' revenue-generating enterprises. The MIS system tracks target employees' use of various social services at the time of hire and tracks changes in use of services every

TRANSFORMING CHARITY

SROI Report · Winter 2000

KEY SOCIAL IMPACT FINDINGS
Select Results from the Youth Industry Employee Survey

Enterprise employees participated in face-to-face interviews at the time of hire (baseline) and six months later (follow-up) to assess their experience of change in the areas of employment, income, housing stability, use of public assistance, use of social services, criminal justice involvement, and other barriers to employment. For each outcome area, the employees' experience six months before hire (baseline) is compared with their experience six months before follow-up. The results below reflect key findings on the social impacts based on the responses of Youth Industry's enterprise employees, including Einstein's Cafe, Nu2U/Nu2U2, Pedal Revolution and Recycled Merchandise. Only statistically significant changes and changes reflecting an impact among more than 20% of the interviewed employees are included.

EMPLOYMENT
96% of respondents experienced a real increase in monthly income from work from their time of hire to their time of follow-up. The average amount of increase was $907.

BARRIERS TO EMPLOYMENT
41% of respondents had been convicted of a crime prior to being hired at YI. Only 14% were convicted of a crime (including drug possession) in the six months before follow-up.

SUBSTANCE USE
At follow-up those respondents using "harder drugs" are more likely to be homeless (67%) or at risk of homelessness (39%) than in a stable home (20%).

HOUSING
44% of respondents experienced an increase in the stability of their housing situation while 17% remained in a stable home. 33% stayed at risk for homelessness, and 6% experienced a decline in their housing stability.

PUBLIC ASSISTANCE AND SERVICE UTILIZATION
While 32% of respondents received some form of public assistance in the six months before baseline, this decreased to only 11% at follow-up. The most common form of public assistance utilization at both baseline and follow-up was Food Stamps.

PSYCHO-SOCIAL CHARACTERISTICS
From baseline to follow-up, 24% of respondents' level of social support increased.

SATISFACTION WITH YI PROGRAMS
97% of YI employees interviewed said they would recommend YI programs to a friend or family member seeking vocational services.

"...(Youth Industry) has given me a second chance, numerous chances, made me realize people can change...." — YI EMPLOYEE

Figure C

148

six months for the next 2 years. Not only does the MIS provide a profile of the target employee of each enterprise, but the change data drives the social purpose value calculated in the SROI analysis. The data from the MIS system is combined with enterprise results as well as new taxes paid to generate the SROI Reports.

Such MIS investment is not cheap. REDF has had the luxury of funding its own MIS development, which most nonprofits could not afford. Many foundations are either oblivious to the advantages of such an MIS system or unwilling to pay for it. And yet, no sustainable social sector performance culture can exist without investment in similar technology. This presents an opportunity for philanthropic and even governmental initiatives. Benson testifies firsthand that the trouble with performing ROI analyses on human services agencies often resides in the difficulty of finding and organizing data. This is because his analysis is performed by working with data systems designed and used without any consistent ROI concept in mind. The opportunity for foundations and public agencies is twofold: first, they can finance a broader social sector ROI project that attempts to define "industry standards" based on the helpful start of Benson, REDF, and others engaged in similar work; second, they can invest in the technological capacity needed to make the use of these industry ROI standards possible.

Once these three points are considered—that we can and should begin to bridge the gap between our markets and our social missions, that we have the capability of creating and living by much higher social-sector-performance standards, and that we need the technological investment to make those new performance standards "come to life" in everyday practice—we can begin to see other possibilities for transforming charity in ever new ways.

Local geographic information systems used by municipal planners could begin to incorporate social-purpose investment information in their databases, which would help philanthropists and public officials see where investment is needed and how current investment is faring. This might foster unhealthy competition between local social purpose organizations, but it would also likely foster new collaborations and motivate new philanthropic ventures that focus more intensively on results. Services for the nonprofit marketplace, such as Guidestar (www.guidestar.com), which contains comprehensive data on nonprofits for donors, and SF Reports (www.sf.org), whose mission is to facilitate communication between donors and nonprofits through standard-form reporting, could begin to include performance information—much like any of the myriad Internet resources for our financial capital markets, which contain performance data on publicly traded companies. This would help the general public in its philanthropic investment decision-making. It might also help temper the current enthusiasm over e-philanthropy—or the use of the Internet for raising money for charities—so that it does not merely become a new version of intention-based charity for the twenty-first century.[27] Also, an accurate and generally accepted standard for taxpayer savings resulting from the interventions of human services should guide policy makers in finding ways to make those savings "real." When a particular city or region has a high SROI due to a forward-looking and effective human services network, it should be able to realize the savings it has generated in the form of a general purpose grant to be reinvested back into the community. Or the organizations largely responsible for the savings should be rewarded with microgrants or development capital. The list of possibilities could go on.

Conclusion

Like Chapters Two and Three, the present chapter does not pretend to exhaust its subject matter. Chapter Two examined three examples of improving nonprofit capacity to help people transition into independence according to market-based principles, practices, and partnerships. A number of other organizations could have been examined instead, and a variety of public policy topics could have been discussed. But the three examples were chosen to depict a continuum of relationships that demonstrate different levels at which the mission meets the market.

Likewise, Chapter Three could have placed its attention on CDCs and performance contracting, which it only briefly treated. It could have focused upon community-based, secondary financial markets. Even the three pillars of civic infrastructure discussed in Chapter Three could have grown to ten pillars and included other community-building institutions and tools. The chapter concentrated instead upon the role of intermediaries in building FBO networks, because the topic is popular and yet lacks guidance, and because it holds great promise and yet is underutilized.

The present chapter could have focused upon a host of nonprofit capacity-building strategies and tools. Or it could have performed case studies on public agencies that have responded to new performance standards. Or it could have cataloged the many examples of outcome measurement being used across the country by social sector organizations. Instead it concentrated exclusively on ROI and the possibility it offers the social sector, because without it, future attempts to responsibly account for our social sector spending and activity will be, at best, second-best. And if we care about the beneficiaries of charitable services, then we owe them better accounting practices for the services they receive. For-profit corporations that routinely deliver poor-quality service to customers will be held accountable (and will go out of business) regardless of their intentions. Why should social service organizations that underserve their customers be continually justified by their intentions? It is hardly charitable to protect bureaucratic and unresponsive organizations, public or private, that consistently fail to serve people well. Without better, generally accepted standards, we will have no way of knowing whether or not America's $1 trillion social sector is actually helping people the best it can.

New Ways

Why do the topics and examples in this book constitute transforming charity? As was said in Chapter One, the wake of welfare reform has demanded that we find new sources of economic opportunity and independence for people, new ways of leveraging community assets such as FBOs and enterprising nonprofits, and new ways of assessing the value that is created in the process. As individuals and organizations across the nation engage in these new ways of assisting poor and low-income families, they are changing the practice of charity in America. They are changing the way that we view the institutions of charity, and they are changing how we think about what serves people well.

In the first place, the new ways of charity are showing us that a multisector social sector is the future of charity. The case studies in Chapters Two and Three showed effective compassion through multisector partnerships. The all too familiar argument about whether the public or private sector should assume the main responsibility for the poor is becoming more and more vacuous, or at least artificial. At the local level, which is the only level at which charity is truly delivered, it hardly makes sense to assist the poor from within the confines of one sector alone. This does not mean, however, that each sector can do the other sectors' jobs. Religious charity, for instance, could never be replicated by a secular organization. The task for individual cities and communities is to bring all the key stakeholders together to address real problems with real collaborations rooted in what representatives from each sector do best. Public officials should bring members of the nonprofit and business communities to the table at the "front-end" of policy design, not at the "back-end" where each sector has a government program dumped on it accompanied by instructions to "collaborate." Likewise, a group of churches committed to tackling the affordable housing issue in their communities should bring local housing agency officials into their planning early enough to make sure they are aware of all possible financing objectives and not replicating some other group's work.

The public square is a complex place. In medieval and early modern cities, it was a place where a person, rich or poor, went to have multiple needs and interests met. Religious, commercial, civic, and recreational options existed in one place. Today's public square is far more complex because it is far less geographically defined. However, the more we can coordinate the activity of multiple sectors around an issue or problem, the better we will serve the spiritual, economic, material, and emotional needs that people have. For those excluded from the economic and civic mainstream, how successful we are on this front may make the difference in their future.

Next, the new ways of charity are showing us that an investment-based, rather than intention-based, strategy focuses our charitable work on value cre-

ation, which is good for the beneficiaries of charity. Value creation, as this chapter has shown, can be understood as reduced dependence on someone else's money, increased reliance on one's own income, and an increased contribution to society. It can also be understood as the improved likelihood that services will increase someone's social capital and reduce the likelihood of incarcerations, victimizations by crime, out-of-wedlock child births, school drop-outs, and so on. Chapters Two through Four have given examples of groups doing what it takes to live up to the responsibility of helping people. Helping people change their positions in their social networks so that they are more likely to succeed is far more important than merely delivering "compassion" that is well-intentioned but looks to nothing other than relieving immediate needs. Intentions matter, as do immediate needs, but our conventional institutions of charity place too much importance on them. Politicians may repeatedly speak of investments in education and job training, but in so far as they offer no systemic reforms that demand real results, their words are meaningless. The same goes for foundations, philanthropists, and charities. The new ways of charity are born of an impatience with such duplicitous word-wrangling.

All investment-based charity looks at results not processes; ends first, means second. Intention-based charity is really crueler than one may think. It looks at failure with a compassionate shrug of the shoulders and remarks, "We tried—sorry." Investment-based charity aims at changed lives, measurable results, and does whatever must be done, however alarming, in order to succeed. It says to the poor, "Friend, you won't go without hope in my house," and allocates resources, forms partnerships, and makes demands of itself and those it serves in order to live up to its promise.

Where Do the New Ways Take Us?

The future of charitable activity—and the social sector generally—will continue its process of transformation the more it brings greater rationality and coherence to its practices. This does not necessarily mean it needs a headquarters or a centralized system of operation, though the emergence of several social sector "clusters" in America would probably be a great service to social sector activity. Clusters such as these would be what the Silicon Valley is to high-tech and what Hartford, Connecticut, is to insurance. A social sector cluster would gather together philanthropic trade associations and publications, philanthropic services, money management services, and social sector research and Internet services.

But regardless of whether or not these clusters arise, the social sector would bring greater rationality and coherence to its practices through the following three developments.

1. *Networks of Intermediaries.* Chapter Three focuses upon a couple of intermediaries that help to leverage the strength of FBOs for the good of the community. But intermediary organizations can serve a wider range of organizations and interests and should be taken seriously in a world of transforming charity. In fact, it is reasonable to expect that as intermediaries grow into their role as hubs of social sector activity they will gain a new institutional place and authority in American civic life. They help create local change out of global ideas and resources. They can convert information and resources, to which smaller service providers do not have access, into programs those smaller providers can deliver. And by "sitting" between those providers and larger governmental, philanthropic, and economic institutions, they help protect the character and integrity of the smaller organizations whose effectiveness rests precisely on the fact that they are not big.

   Intermediaries could be like Good Samaritan in Ottawa County. They may be a newly formed organization in one community, a foundation in another, or a large church in yet another. A community may have several intermediaries. And, as James Q. Wilson's proposal, cited in Chapter Three, suggests, we may be well-served by a national intermediary specifically for FBOs. Intermediaries are and should remain diverse. But through a more highly focused and dedicated approach among local officials and community leaders than is currently practiced, intermediary organizations could become new "centers" to social sector activity that is increasingly without a center. Public agencies can help this process by identifying likely intermediaries for delivering their services, and foundations, which often only fund direct service delivery because it is "sexier," should think long and hard about working through intermediaries to maximize impact in their communities.

2. *Standardized criteria for assessing impact.* This chapter has focused upon ROI models as one way of standardizing results. I said above that there are other ways to focus upon value creation, and these should also be pursued. In order to develop the forums for an ongoing conversation about what social ROI should look like, foundations and public agencies have to get involved more proactively than they are at present. Akin to funding intermediaries, funding outcomes measurement is not regarded as sexy. But if done properly, it may make the greatest difference in the future. The word *standards* often creates discomfort among public and private sector leaders because it sounds too much like an iron jacket placed upon the soft and fluid nature of social sector work. Attempts to quantify unquantifiable social phenomena should indeed be abandoned. But services that either promote or end dependency and foster independence are not soft matters. Very real indicators of success can be examined and assessed. We simply need more people to spend more time working through the meaning of these issues and develop tools to help the assessment process.

3. *Improved "connectivity" between social sector players.* The various sectors of society—business, government, nonprofit—do not exist independently by nature. "Sectors" are largely creations of the federal government for accounting purposes, and the past

fifty years have seen institutional practices follow these creations. During this time, government became less a custodian of the public square and more a deliverer of services. Financial institutions increasingly disregarded community development as related to their missions, and nonprofits began their own trade groups and began holding their own conferences. As this book has shown, the activities of these various players in social sector and charitable matters can and do overlap in ways now considered unconventional.

New "collision" points are needed in communities where members of business, government, and nonprofit organizations run into each other—that is, where they interact and address problems together. Partnerships and organizations such as those featured in this book, or numerous other multisector collaborative arrangements across the nation, are the products of visionary leadership. Because our various sectors do in fact operate relatively independently today, nothing short of leadership will change that. There exists great opportunity for well-financed retired (or semiretired) entrepreneurs to create environments where multisector leadership is brought together to form problem-solving coalitions. Opportunity also exists for an entrepreneurial spirit within a variety of public agencies to form and fund coalitions whose job it is to create results not just administer another program. Consider the State of Florida's welfare-to-work program, WAGES, which was formed as an independent organization in Tampa, away from the government culture of Tallahassee, and headed up by a private sector chairman. Its mission was to drive itself out of business by getting Florida's welfare population working. It created more than twenty public-private coalitions across the state, funded them, and charged them with dropping their welfare caseloads by helping people find productive employment. Florida has been the most successful of the nation's largest states in moving its welfare population to work—

so successful, in fact, that WAGES has lived up to its charge and is now out of business. The state's workforce agency now has the task of building up a viable generation of workers throughout the state.

WAGES created collision points between people unaccustomed to working together. It brought private-sector business acumen to a publicly funded process. It devolved decision-making over public funds to coalitions whose private sector members had just as much say as the public officials as to how the funds would be used. And economically troubled families benefited as a result. What else is the public square in today's world than this kind of cooperation between different sectors for the good of all? And how else will the public square grow more robust if it is not driven by leaders able to see beyond the narrow confines of today's overly sectored world?

If connectivity between social sector stakeholders is to be improved, we will also need better networks between those that have resources and those that deliver services. Online services that create a better informed donor base, such as www.guidestar.com, are a start. But a host of additional tools are needed to assist donors and charities with their communication and their joint strategic planning for achieving results. Money managers who are often disconnected from the actual philanthropic intent of their clients would be well-served by tools that help them regularly direct resources to social purpose organizations in ways that satisfy the donors. And publicly sponsored access to geographic information systems would help community-based public and philanthropic planning achieve real results.

The future of transformed charity may be our past. The overall effort by those walking upon the new ways of the social sector can be seen as an attempt to recover the long-revered American practice of joining our highest economic and moral ideals. In the words of sociologist Robert Wuthnow:

> *The American Dream is a moral framework. It encourages people to work hard, giving them hope that their work will be rewarded . . . By the end of the nineteenth century a significant alteration in the American Dream was taking place. New scientific conceptions of work and money were being advanced by political economists, making it more difficult to integrate moral considerations into formal discussions of economic life . . . [T]oday, much of the moral strength embedded in the American Dream remains intact. To think of it as a moral framework, however, has become less common. Much of the recent literature uses the term to mean little more than the desire to own a home or to frame arguments about the aspirations of minority groups for economic equality. Economistic thinking dominates discussions of work and money, while questions of moral commitment, character, and human values seem more difficult to relate to economic behavior.*[28]

Transforming charity requires that nontraditional partners from a variety of society's sectors work together to make the American Dream really work for everyone. Only through their efforts will our moral and economic frameworks become part of the same framework. Investment-based charity, a new multisector public square, and civic infrastructure are trends that exist on the margins of society, though they serve mainstream interests. To become mainstream, they require leaders with imagination, vision, and courage.

CHAPTER FOUR

Endnotes

1 *Nonprofit Sector Size and Scope*, Nonprofit Information Center, Independent Sector (Washington, D.C.: 2000).
2 Only Germany, France, the UK, Italy, and Spain have larger GNPs than the amount of money that the United States spends in the nonprofit sector. Spain's GNP is roughly the same as America's nonprofit spending, and France's, the UK's, and Italy's domestic economies are each only roughly twice as large.
3 *United States' Nonprofits by Type*, National Center for Charitable Statistics, 1997.
4 "IRS Is Too Lax in Screening Nonprofit Groups, Critics Say," *Atlanta Journal-Constitution*, October 24, 2000.
5 *The U.S. Budget for Fiscal Year 2001, Historical Tables*, U.S. Office of Management and Budget.
6 U.S. Census Bureau, "Federal Government Finances and Employment," *Statistical Abstract of the United States*, 1999, 350.
7 John J. Havens and Paul G. Schervish, *Millionaires and the Millennium: New Estimates of the Forthcoming Wealth Transfer and the Prospects for a Golden Age of Philanthropy* (Boston: Social Welfare Research Institute, 1999), 1.
8 Michael Porter and Mark Kramer, "Philanthropy's New Agenda: Creating Value," *Harvard Business Review* (November-December 1999), 122.
9 Karl Taro Greenfeld and David S. Jackson, "Venture Philanthropists," *Time* (July 24, 2000), 55.
10 Christopher Swope, "Robert Rubin's Urban Crusade," *Governing* (August 2000).
11 Porter and Kramer, 125.
12 Peter Frumkin, "Evaluating for Success: And the Five Dimensions of Philanthropic Impact," *Philanthropy* (September-October 1999), 10–11.
13 http://www.gsb.stanford.edu/csi/csi_about.html
14 One writer claims that such programs have increased 500 percent in the past decade. See Paul Sturm, "The Seven Rules of Successful Collaboration," *Nonprofit World*, vol. 18, no. 2 (March-April 2000), 33–36.
15 Severyn Bruyn, *Civil Economy: Transforming the Market in the Twenty-First Century* (Ann Arbor: University of Michigan Press, 2000). My thanks to Paul Brooks for introducing me to Bruyn's work and for walking me through the significance of several of the concepts contained within it.
16 Jed Emerson, "The Nature of Returns: A Social Capital Markets Inquiry into Elements of Investment and the Blended Value Proposition," Social Enterprise Series, no. 17 (Boston: Harvard Business School, 2000).
17 Quoted in William Ryan, "The New Landscape for Nonprofits," *Harvard*

Business Review (January-February 1999), 132.
18. Dennis Benson, *Return on Inve$tment: Guidelines to Determine Workforce Development Impact* (Worthington, OH: Appropriate Solutions, Inc., 1999), 9–10.
19. Ibid., 11.
20. The multiplier that is used is a product of perhaps the two most sophisticated studies on long-term employment training impact: Lee Lillard and Hong Tan, *Private Sector Training: Who Gets It and What Are Its Effects?* (Santa Monica, CA: The Rand Corporation, 1986), and Richard Moore, Daniel Blake, and Michael Phillips, *Accounting for Training: An Analysis of the Outcomes of California Employment Training Panel Programs* (Northridge, CA: School of Business Administration, California State University, 1995).
21. Benson, 11–12, 61.
22. Quoted, with minor modifications, from Jed Emerson and Jay Wachowicz, *Social Return on Investment: Exploring Aspects of Value Creation in the Nonprofit Sector* (San Francisco: REDF, 1999), 9.
23. Ibid., 5.
24. The reader is encouraged to see REDF's paper *SROI Methodology* (published Q1 2001) in order to see the graphic representation of these points in a sample enterprise.
25. See, for instance, his paper, again with Jay Wachowicz, *Riding on the Bleeding Edge: A Framework for Tracking Equity in the Social Sector and the Creation of a Nonprofit Stock Market* (San Francisco: REDF, 2000).
26. Complete SROI Reports on all of REDF's portfolio enterprises can be obtained from REDF's website at www.redf.org.
27. For a report on the explosion of *e-philanthropy and a catalog of over 140 existing philanthropy-related websites*, see the Kellogg Foundation's *e-Philanthropy, Volunteerism, and Social Changemaking: A New Landscape of Resources, Issues, and Opportunities* (February 2000).
28. Robert Wuthnow, *Poor Richard's Principle: Recovering the American Dream through the Moral Dimension of Work, Business, and Money* (Princeton: Princeton University Press, 1996), 4–5.

ABOUT HUDSON INSTITUTE

Hudson Institute is a private, not-for-profit research organization founded in 1961 by the late Herman Kahn. Hudson analyzes and makes recommendations about public policy for business and government executives, as well as for the public at large. The institute does not advocate an express ideology or political position. However, more than thirty years of work on the most important issues of the day has forged a viewpoint that embodies skepticism about the conventional wisdom, optimism about solving problems, a commitment to free institutions and individual responsibility, an appreciation of the crucial role of technology in achieving progress, and an abiding respect for the importance of values, culture, and religion in human affairs.

Since 1984, Hudson has been headquartered in Indianapolis, Indiana. It also maintains offices in Washington, D.C.; Madison, Wisconsin; and Tampa, Florida.

INDEX

Aid to Families with Dependent Children (AFDC): *see* Public assistance

Bain and Company: 22, 132

Benson, Dennis: 138-141, 147, 149

Berger, Peter: 24

Bridge Group, The: 22

Bruyn, Severyn: 133

Bush, George W.: 96, 97

Cannon, Carl: 53

Capacity-building: 53, 55, 68, 70-72, 73, 75-76, 78, 79, 80, 82, 98-99, 102, 110, 113, 116-117, 131, 132-133, 136, 149, 150, 151

Capitalism: see Market economy, opportunity

Carlyle, Thomas: 53-54

Casey Foundation: 118

Center for Public Justice: 95

Charitable Choice: 25, 29, 93, 95, 116

Charity: 9-12, 18-19, 20, 21, 39, 51, 53, 56, 65, 87, 91, 92, 109, 115, 119, 127-128, 130 133, 135, 136, 147, 149, 152, 151-158

giving: 15, 18-19, 32, 36, 38, 39, 40-41, 52, 130

intention-based charity: 9-11, 12, 16, 18-19, 20, 22, 38, 39, 40, 41, 43, 74-75, 109, 127, 130, 134, 150, 151, 152-153

investment-based charity: *see* Results

transforming charity: defined, 20-22; 12, 18, 26, 27, 30 34, 35, 38, 41, 43-44, 87, 91, 119, 130, 133, 135, 149, 151, 154, 158

tzedakah: 9

Chaves, Mark: 102

Chicago Christian Industrial League (CCIL): 66-70, 72

Church, Vicky: 60, 61

Civic engagement: *see* Social capital

Civic infrastructure: 12, 29, 45, 85-92, 97, 115-122, 151, 158

Civil society: 11, 12, 22, 23-33, 44, 110

Clinton, Bill: 96

Cnaan, Ram: 96

Collins, Jim: 22

Community-based organizations: 11, 12, 18, 19, 24-25, 26, 27, 31, 34, 42-43, 45-46, 86-87, 89, 93, 95, 97-98, 99, 108, 113, 118, 134

Community Development Block Grants: 122

Community development corporations (CDCs): 26, 86, 87-89, 90, 93, 118, 130, 150

Community Vocational Enterprises (CVE): 77-79

Coleman, James: 40

Dees, Gregory: 52

De Young, Janet: 105, 106

DiIulio, John: 94

Dionne, E.J.: 97

Doerr, John: 130

Drucker, Peter: 31, 32

Earned Income Tax Credit: 44, 91, 92, 141

Elias, Jaan: 52

Emden, Germany: 15-19, 53, 115

Emerson, Jed: 133, 142, 144

European Union: 128

Faith-based organizations (FBOs): 20, 25, 26, 86-88, 90, 92-98, 99-101, 102, 110, 112, 113, 115-118, 119, 127, 138, 151, 154

Fidelity Investment's Charitable Gift Fund: 35

First Amendment issues: 90, 97, 100, 106, 115-116

Ford, Henry: 51

Ford Foundation: 35

Foundations: *see* Philanthropy

Front Porch Alliance (FPA): 99, 109-115

Frumkin, Peter: 131

Gates Foundation, Bill and Melinda: 35

INDEX

Goldsmith, Stephen: 99, 110, 111, 113

Good Samaritan Ministries: 102-109, 115, 116, 120, 154

Goodwill Industries: 63

Gore, Al: 96

Government: 10, 12, 19, 20, 23, 26, 26-30, 31, 32, 43, 46, 57, 80-82, 86, 87, 89, 90, 95-97, 98-100, 101, 109 ff., 114-115, 116, 117, 118

    government agencies: 10, 19, 21, 26, 41, 43, 45, 46, 52, 53, 73, 80, 82, 87, 88, 89, 90, 93, 96, 98, 102, 112, 116, 117, 119, 120, 135, 149, 151, 155, 156

    government spending: 35, 36-37, 41-42, 52, 81-82, 87, 92, 115-116, 122, 131, 134-135

Grossman, Allen: 22, 74

Guidestar: 150, 157

Harvard University: 132, 133

    Social Enterprise Initiative: 132

    Hauser Center for Nonprofit Organizations: 132

Havens, John: 36, 129

Hudson Institute: 32, 95

Independent Sector: 37, 95, 105

Individual development accounts (IDAs): 26

Intermediary organizations: 12, 45-46, 85, 86, 89, 90, 93, 96, 97, 98-101, 102, 103, 105, 106, 108, 109-110, 115-118, 151, 154-155

Jackson, Noel: 67, 69

Job Training Partnership Act: 138

Jobs Partnership: 54, 55, 57-63, 74, 80, 86, 120

Kramer, Mark: 130, 131

Letts, Christine: 21, 74

Local Initiative Support Corporation (LISC): 89, 130

Low-income families and individuals: 9, 10, 11, 12, 16-17, 18, 19, 20-21, 23-24, 25, 26, 27, 29, 30, 33, 35, 36, 40-45, 51, 52, 53-54, 56, 57, 80, 85, 90, 91-92, 94-95, 98, 106, 119, 122, 132, 134, 135, 136, 137, 140-141, 151

Lowi, Theodore: 29

Mangum, Chris: 57, 62, 63

165

Market economy, opportunity: 12, 33, 45, 51-53, 53-57, 64, 65, 69, 74, 75, 82, 91, 115, 121

McCoy, Donald: 57

Mentoring: 9, 40, 55, 58-59, 59-60, 61, 103, 104-106, 107, 108, 111, 121, 138

Morris, Dick: 31, 32

Moynihan, Daniel Patrick: 29

Multisector collaboration: 26-33, 45, 87, 92, 119-122, 127, 152, 156, 158

Neuhaus, Richard John: 24

Nisbet, Robert: 24

Nonprofit organizations: 11, 21-22, 26-27, 29, 30, 32, 34, 35-37, 38, 44, 45, 46, 51-54, 56, 64, 65, 73, 75, 76, 80, 81, 82, 86, 97, 102, 119, 127-128, 132, 133, 134, 136

Omidyar, Pierre: 39

Paul, St.: 56

Partnerships: *see* Multisector collaboration

Performance contracting: 86-90, 118, 119-120

Philanthropy: 10, 12, 21, 28, 33, 35-41, 45, 51-52, 74, 76, 80, 120, 129, 130-131, 149-150, 153, 155

Pioneer Human Services: 63-64

Porter, Michael: 130, 131

Poverty: *see* Low-income families and individuals

Public assistance (food stamps, housing vouchers, cash assistance, child care, transportation): 23-24, 37, 44, 45, 61, 85, 92, 97, 103, 120, 139, 140

  Aid to Families with Dependent Children (AFDC): 121

  Temporary Assistance to Needy Families (TANF): 122

Putnam, Robert: 40, 42

Randolph, Isaac: 114-115

Reagan, Ronald: 93

Results: 9-11, 12, 19-22, 35, 38, 40, 41, 44, 46, 69-70, 80, 82, 89-90, 91, 93, 96, 110, 122, 127, 130, 133, 134-135, 141, 144, 147, 149-150, 153, 155, 157

  investment-based charity: 11-12, 35-44, 46-47, 73, 74 ff., 81-82, 114, 127-128, 130-133, 152-153, 158

INDEX

return on investment (ROI): 133-137, 138-141, 151, 155

social return on investment (SROI): 141-150

Return on Investment: *see* Results

Rivers, Eugene: 111

Roberts Enterprise Development Fund (REDF): 54, 55, 56, 74-79, 80, 82, 120, 121, 141-150

Rockefeller Foundation: 118

Rubin, Robert: 89

Ryan, William: 21, 74

Schervish, Paul: 36, 129

Self-sufficiency: 9, 11, 16, 18, 24, 45, 46, 51, 52, 53, 56, 65, 66, 70, 80, 104-105, 109, 116, 118, 119, 127, 129, 136-137, 144, 150, 151, 155

ServiceMaster Corporation: 54, 55, 56, 63-73, 74, 80, 119, 120

   Work Training Businesses: 63-73

SF Reports: 150

Social capital: 40-44, 46-47, 85, 86, 131-132, 153

   civic engagement: 17, 25, 27, 30, 36, 40, 44, 85, 87

Social entrepreneurship: 21, 33, 51-53, 132

Social return on investment (SROI): *see* Results

Social sector: 20, 21, 27-33, 35-36, 38, 42, 43-44, 46, 51, 52, 56, 73, 77, 79-80, 82, 118-122, 127-129, 131-133, 137, 144, 147, 149, 151-152, 153-158

Social Security (FICA): 36, 128, 139, 140

Stanczykiewicz, Bill: 110

Temporary Assistance to Needy Families (TANF): *see* Public assistance

Ten Point Coalition: 111, 114

Tierney, Thomas J.: 22

Toqueville, Alexis de: 31

Urban Institute: 118

U.S. Department of Commerce: 140

U.S. Department of Defense: 128

U.S. Department of Health and Human Services: 128, 135

U.S. Department of Housing and Urban Development: 108, 118, 128, 135

U.S. Department of Labor: 32, 128, 135

U.S. Treasury: 128

U.S. General Accounting Office (GAO): 41-42

Vives, Juan Luis: 16

Wachowicz, Jay: 142

Walters, John: 36

Welfare (see Public assistance)

Welfare reform: 17, 18-26, 28, 29, 33, 36, 43, 56, 30, 39, 93, 103, 108, 109, 115, 118-119, 122, 139, 151

Personal Responsibility and Work Opportunity Reconciliation Act (welfare reform act): 23, 25, 43, 93, 122

Welfare-to-Work Partnership: 32-33

Wheeler Enterprises: 71

White, James: 63

White House Office of Faith-Based and Community Initiatives: 97

Wilson, James Q.: 99, 154

Workforce Investment Act (WIA): 28-29, 43, 81, 138

Wuthnow, Robert: 158

URBAN CHURCH
LEADERSHIP CENTER
3000 Leonard NE - 2nd Level/GRTS
Grand Rapids, MI 49525